THE MILITARY HISTORICAL SOCIETY

SPECIAL NUMBER
1994

OFFICERS' WAIST BELT CLASPS
1855 – 1902

by
Lelia B. Ryan, BA

Published by
The Military Historical Society
c/o The National Army Museum
Royal Hospital Road
Chelsea
London SW3 4HT

Copyright 1994
L. B. Ryan

All rights reserved. No part of this book may be reproduced or transmitted in copy form or by any means electronic or mechanical, including photo-copying, recording for any information storage and retrieval system, without the permission of the Society and the Author.

British Library Cataloguing in Publication Data.
A catalogue record for this book is available from the British Library.

ISBN 0 9510603 2 5

Printed in England by Arrow Press, Farnham, Surrey GU9 7UG

ACKNOWLEDGEMENTS

I am deeply grateful to many friends who, through the years, have been so generous with photographs, photocopies, sketches, notes, and access to their collections. Among the many are: Mr Douglas N. Anderson, Mr J. W. Atkin, Major R. W. Bennett, BSc(Eng), CEng, MIMechE, Mr W. Y. Carman, FRHistS, FSA, FSA (Scot), Field Marshal Sir John Chapple, GCB, CBE, MA, FZS, FRGS, FLS, Messrs K. R. A. Gibbs, R. G. Harris, C. Housley, and H. L. King, the late Mr A. L. Kipling, Lieutenant Colonel C. P. Love, TD, Mr Charles Quinn, Professor Charles Thomas, CBE, DL, DLitt, FBA, FSA, the late Admiral W. G. Whiteside, OBE, USN, and Colonel D. R. Wood.

I am also very grateful indeed to my editor, Colonel D. R. Wood, for being so helpful and for so patiently and tactfully coping with me and the trials of overseas mail.

I must thank the following for permission to use their material in my research: Army Museums Ogilby Trust, Colonel P. S. Walton, Secretary, and Major J. J. Falkner; The Durham Light Infantry and Arts Centre; D. Endean Ivall and Charles Thomas (*Military Insignia of Cornwall*, Penwith Books in Association with The Duke of Cornwall's Light Infantry Regimental Museum, 1974); *Journal of the Society for Army Historical Research*, Mr M. A. Cane, Honorary Editor, and Brigadier T. F. J. Collins, CBE, DL; the National Army Museum, and particularly Dr P. B. Boyden, PhD, BA, and Miss Clare Wright, BA; the Sussex Combined Services Museum; Messrs Wallis & Wallis and Mr S. R. Butler; and the West Sussex Record Office.

And last, I owe a continuing debt of gratitude to my late father, Lieutenant Colonel Sidney G. Brady, who started me in collecting, and to my husband, Douglas, who always gives me encouragement and support.

INTRODUCTION

by

Field Marshal Sir John Chapple, GCB, CBE,
President,
The Military Historical Society

Mrs Lelia Ryan has produced an extremely comprehensive work on the officers' waist belt clasps worn by the line infantry between 1855 and 1902. It is greatly enhanced by no less than 241 of her own splendid line drawings which illustrate every clasp described in the text. This is an area of research which has never been done before and about which little is known and even less recorded. It adds a substantial amount to our knowledge in this field, and throws some interesting light on the dress distinctions of the Regiments both before and after Cardwell.

The difficulty of digging out the data to compile this record is immense. It is a tribute to the tenacity of Mrs Ryan that she has succeeded in producing such a full record. There will always be additions and corrections, but I am sure that these will be very few. This work will undoubtedly become the definitive work on this subject. Her achievement is all the more remarkable since she lives in New York. Surely an example to all who research military subjects, and I hope a spur to others to share their knowledge. It is a privilege for The Military Historical Society to be the conduit for this publication.

Gibraltar
1 July 1994

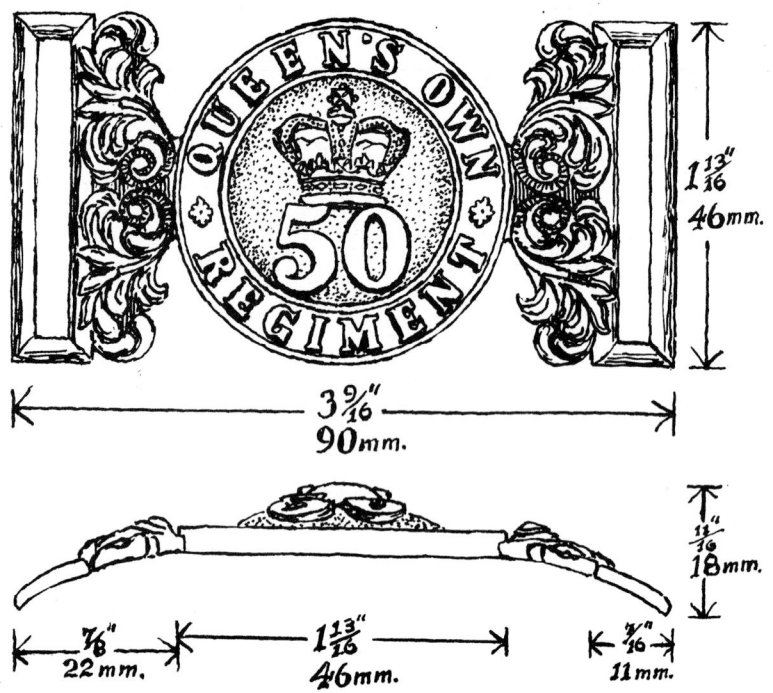

1

2

OFFICERS' WAIST BELT CLASPS 1855-1902

PART I: 1855-1881

When the tunic was introduced in 1855, it was accompanied by a standard waist belt for officers. This replaced the waist belt for field officers, ordered in 1832, and the shoulder belt for officers below field rank. The belt was to be "of enamelled white leather an inch and a half wide," and, say the Dress Regulations of 1855 sternly, "This is to be the only sword belt for all occasions". By 1874, however, the authorities had relented to the point of allowing a gold-lace belt "on state occasions and at balls".

The Dress Regulations of 1855 specify "a round clasp, having on the centre-piece the number of the regiment, surmounted by a crown, both in silver, and on the outer circle the regimental title in silver letters". An example measures 90 mm wide by 46 mm deep. However, different dies and different manufacturers result in differences of a few millimetres, more or less, in either direction. Figure 1 shows a clasp drawn to actual size.

Nothing in the 1855 Dress Regulations indicates special badges or devices on these clasps, but nine years later the 1864 Dress Regulations allow special devices or patterns for twenty-eight regiments — 1st, 2nd, 3rd, 4th, 5th, 6th, 7th, 8th, 9th, 18th, 21st, 23rd, 27th, 41st, 80th, 82nd, 84th, 87th, and 100th to the 109th inclusive. With the possible exception of the 5th Fusiliers (see Figure 9), I have no record of, nor have I ever seen, the crown-over-number clasp for these twenty-eight regiments. I can assume only that the regiments wore these clasps very briefly, if at all, and quickly moved to adopt their particular devices.

Light infantry regiments were to have the bugle horn or French hunting horn in the centre, with the number in the middle. A crown is not mentioned for the light infantry. In addition, the 18th Foot's clasp had the motto of the regiment, VIRTUTIS NAMURCENSIS PRAEMIUM*, on the circle instead of the title, and the 100th Foot substituted a wreath for the title. As a Canadian regiment, it chose a wreath of maple leaves. By 1874, two more regiments, the 65th and 89th, had been added to the list. And certainly more than thirty regiments over the years added devices of various sorts.

In addition to the devices and the variations on the outer circles, changes of regimental titles over twenty-six years, plus different forms of numbers meant many different clasps. For example, the 32nd had as many as four different variations — see Figures 48-51.

The ends of most clasps have a rococo design, as in Figure 1, but some clasps have an oak-leaf and acorn design for the ends as in Figure 148. The acorn-end clasps do not fit together as the rococo ones do, but have a hook on the back, so placed that the end fits neatly.

* "The reward of valour at Namur."

Two regiments had clasps with unusual ends — one of the clasps of the 51st King's Own Light Infantry (Figure 83) and the clasp of the 100th Royal Canadians with maple leaves on the ends (Figure 146). The oak-leaf and acorn ends were used only by the 101st to 109th Regiments, the regiments of the Honourable East India Company.

Soldiers, too, got a new belt for the tunic. Their clasps* were much plainer, made of brass, and bore the regimental title on the circle and the number only in the centre, almost never a device. They were worn only from 1855 to the 1870s when they were replaced by a universal pattern with the Royal Crest in the centre and motto DIEU ET MON DROIT on the circle.

It is usually stated that the titles on the circles of officers' clasps do not include the definite article "The", and that they do on soldiers' clasps. But this is not always the case. See, for example, the officers' clasp of *The Cumberland Regiment* (Figure 54). And there are several soldiers' clasps which lack the article.

With the exception of the special patterns, the clasp has two pieces that interlock, as shown in Figure 2. This leads to the danger for collectors that two mismatched pieces may turn up together. Indeed, I have seen in a catalogue a 95th Foot centre in a West Yorkshire circle. One help in avoiding this sort of put-together clasp is that frequently both pieces will bear the maker's name or the same number — at least an indication that, other things being equal (regimental title and number or device), the clasp is correct.

In dating these clasps, it is helpful to have at hand Parkyn's book on shoulder belt plates°, as he lists all the regimental titles and the dates of changes. If not Parkyn, then a lineage book that will provide the same information. It is obvious that if there is a change in title, a clasp with the new title cannot predate the change.

I have not attempted to cover the Foot Guards or those Scottish regiments wearing dirk belts. Their dirk belt plates and shoulder belt plates are outside the scope of this study. Nor have I covered rifle regiments, whose officers wore black belts, usually under their jackets, without the usual clasps. But I have tried to cover Infantry of the Line, including light infantry and fusiliers.

The 101st to 109th Regiments inclusive, which had been European regiments of the three Presidencies under the Honourable East India Company, became part of the forces of the Crown in 1861. Honourable East India Company regiments usually followed changes in uniform of the British Army, and the European regiments adopted the tunic in 1856 or 1857. This introduced waist belt clasps somewhat similar to the standard pattern, but with their own design elements. I have included illustrations of their clasps prior to 1861 where there is photographic evidence, because

---

*   Described in Equipment Regulations as "Locket, union, regl. pattern."

°   Parkyn, Major H. G., O.B.E. *Shoulder-Belt Plates and Buttons* (Aldershot: Gale & Polden Limited, 1956).

their later special patterns often echoed elements of their earlier clasps. In addition to their oak-leaf and acorn ends, these regiments' clasps lacked the usual title circles, and their centres were larger and more elaborate.

All the devices and badges on the following clasps are silver mounted on gilt centres unless otherwise noted.

1st Foot. The device specified in the 1864 Dress Regulations★ is St Andrew without a number. The first clasp, Figure 3, bears the title THE ROYAL REGIMENT on the circle and St Andrew in the centre. The title dates the clasp from 1855? to 1871. When the title changed in 1871, so did the clasp, as in Figure 4.

2nd Foot. Figure 5 complies with DR 1864 and 1874, but I have no evidence for the use of the title on the circle, except possibly briefly after 1881. However, a photograph of a clasp shows the motto as in Figure 6. The motto° is first specified after 1881 in DR 1883, but it is certainly possible that it was used on the circle prior to 1881.

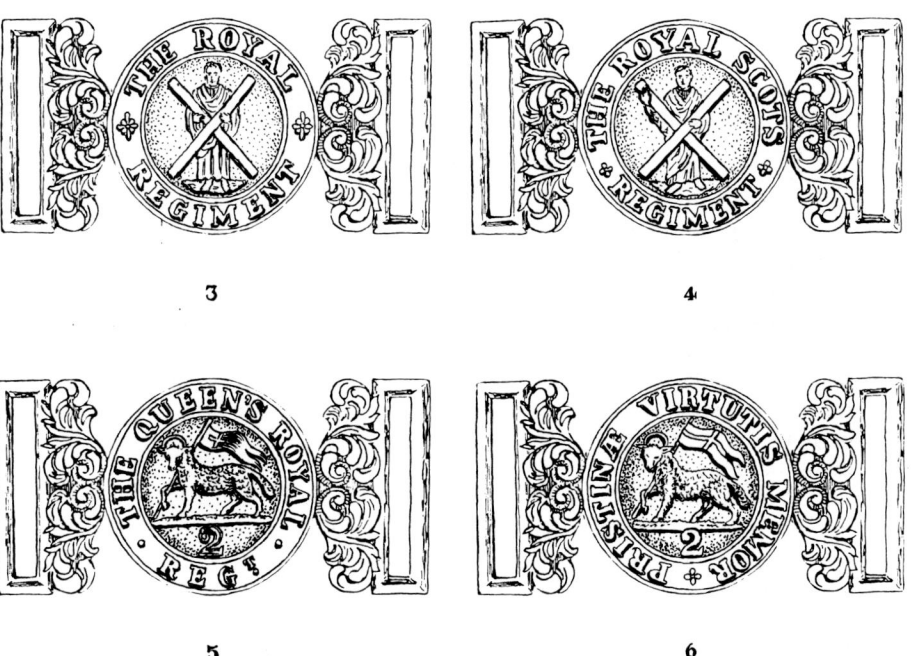

3   4

5   6

★ Hereinafter cited as DR followed by the date.

° PRISTINAE VIRTUTIS MEMOR — "Mindful of former valour."

3rd Foot. Figure 7 conforms to DR 1864 and 1874 and is the only clasp of which I have a record.

4th Foot. Figure 8 conforms to DR 1864 and 1874. The 4th Foot preferred the Roman numeral IV and used it on buttons and shoulder belt plates until 1855 and after that on the officers' waist belt clasps until 1881.

5th Fusiliers. There is an indication that briefly the Regiment's clasp conformed to DR 1855 (Figure 9). Figure 10 shows the clasp specified in DR 1864 and 1874. I have not, however, actually seen either of these clasps or any pictorial evidence of them. So these drawings must be taken as speculation. The 5th, too, preferred the Roman numeral V on badges, buttons, and shoulder belt plates. So I have chosen to show the V on the clasp.

6th Foot. Figure 11 does not match any Dress Regulations, but there is evidence for this clasp. Figure 12 complies with DR 1864 and 1874, but I have no other evidence of this clasp, and therefore it must be taken as speculation.

7th Foot. Figures 13 and 14 differ in the size of the crown and the rose and in the spacing of the title on the circle. Both conform to DR 1864 and DR 1874.

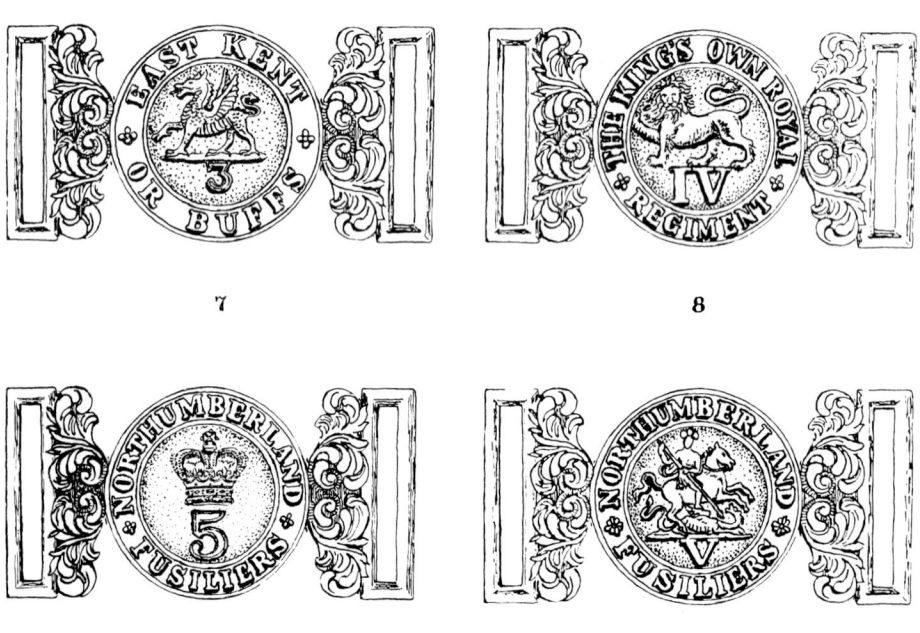

11 12 13 14 15 16

8th Foot. Figure 15 complies with DR 1864 and 1874. Neither, however, mentions the motto★.

9th Foot. Figure 16 also conforms to DR 1864 and 1874.

★ NEC ASPERA TERRENT — "And difficulties do not deter [us]."

17   18

10th Foot. Figure 17, the 10th's clasp, matches DR 1855 — the crown-over-number clasp. It is the first one for which I have photographic evidence. I have no knowledge of a change and believe this was worn until 1881.

11th Foot. Figure 18 is another crown-over-number clasp. Again, there is no evidence of a change before 1881.

12th Foot. Figure 19 conforms to DR 1855, 1864, and 1874. The Regimental History, however, dates this from 1855 to 1872. Figure 20 is said to date from 1872 to 1881; it does not conform to Dress Regulations.*

13th Light Infantry. Dress Regulations call only for light infantry bugle or horn with the number. I have never seen such a clasp for the 13th. But there is evidence for Figure 21, which includes the mural crown with the battle honour JELLALABAD.

14th Foot. Again Dress Regulations specify only the crown and number, but I have seen evidence for Figure 22. The White Horse was an old badge of the 14th.

15th Foot. Figure 23 conforms to Dress Regulations and was probably worn until 1881.

16th Foot. Figure 24 also matches Dress Regulations and probably did not change before 1881.

17th Foot. Figure 25 has the 17th's tiger for service in India and the number, but no crown. Figures 26 and 27 have the crown over tiger over the number. None of these are mentioned in Dress Regulations. I would hazard a guess that 25 was worn first, followed by 26 and/or 27. The devices and title on 26 and 27 agree, but I have included them both since the size of the tiger and crown are different. Even the spacing of the lettering of the titles differs.

* MONTIS INSIGNIA CALPE — "The badge of the Rock, Gibraltar."

19

20

21

22

23

24

25

26

18th Foot. Figure 28 complies with DR 1864, but DR 1874 seem to call for the number below the harp and crown.

19th Foot (Figures 29 and 30) and **20th Foot** (Figure 31). These are standard crown-over-number clasps conforming to DR 1855. I have no evidence of changes prior to 1881.

21st Fusiliers. Figure 32 is as specified in DR 1864 and 1874. This was worn until 1877 when the title changed and the clasp was changed to correspond as shown in Figure 33. This last was worn until 1881.

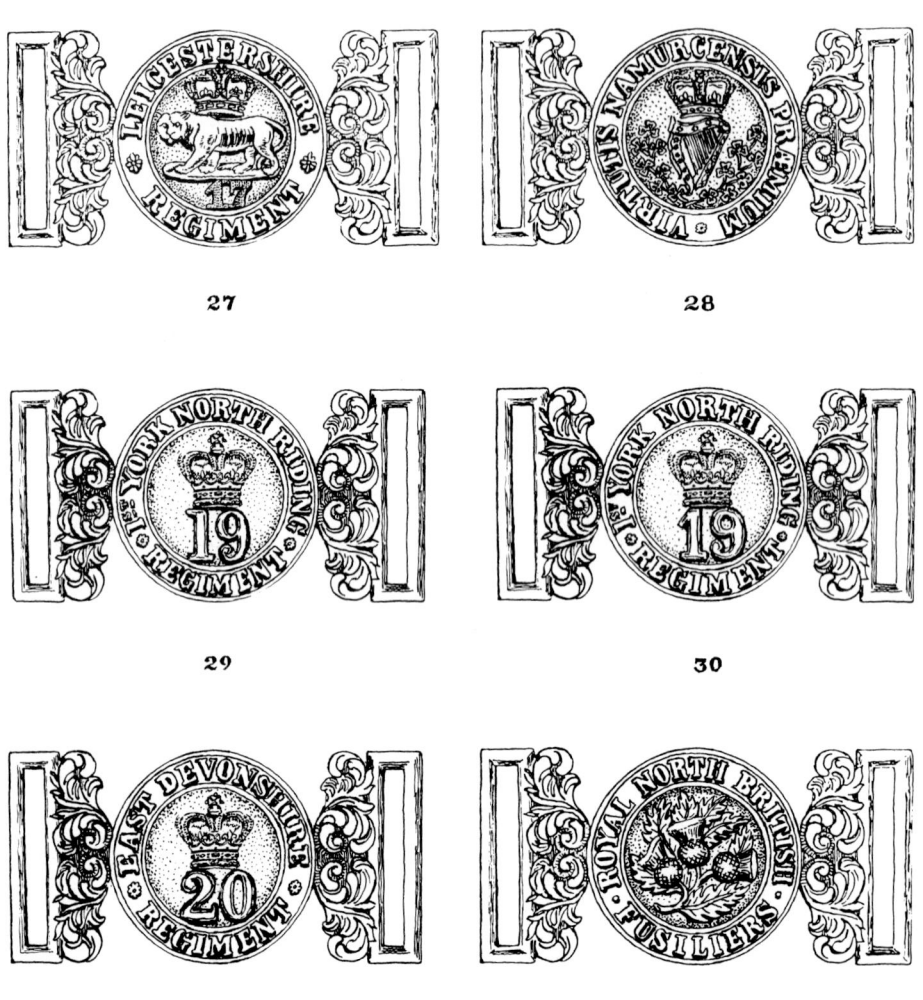

22nd Foot. Figure 34 matches DR 1855 and was worn until 1881.

23rd Fusiliers. DR 1864 and 1874 both specify the Prince of Wales's plumes, but neither mention the number below. Figures 35 and 36 differ in the size of the plumes and numbers.

24th Foot (Figure 37), **25th Foot** (Figure 38), and **26th Foot** (Figure 39) — all comply with DR 1855. To the best of my knowledge there were no changes before 1881.

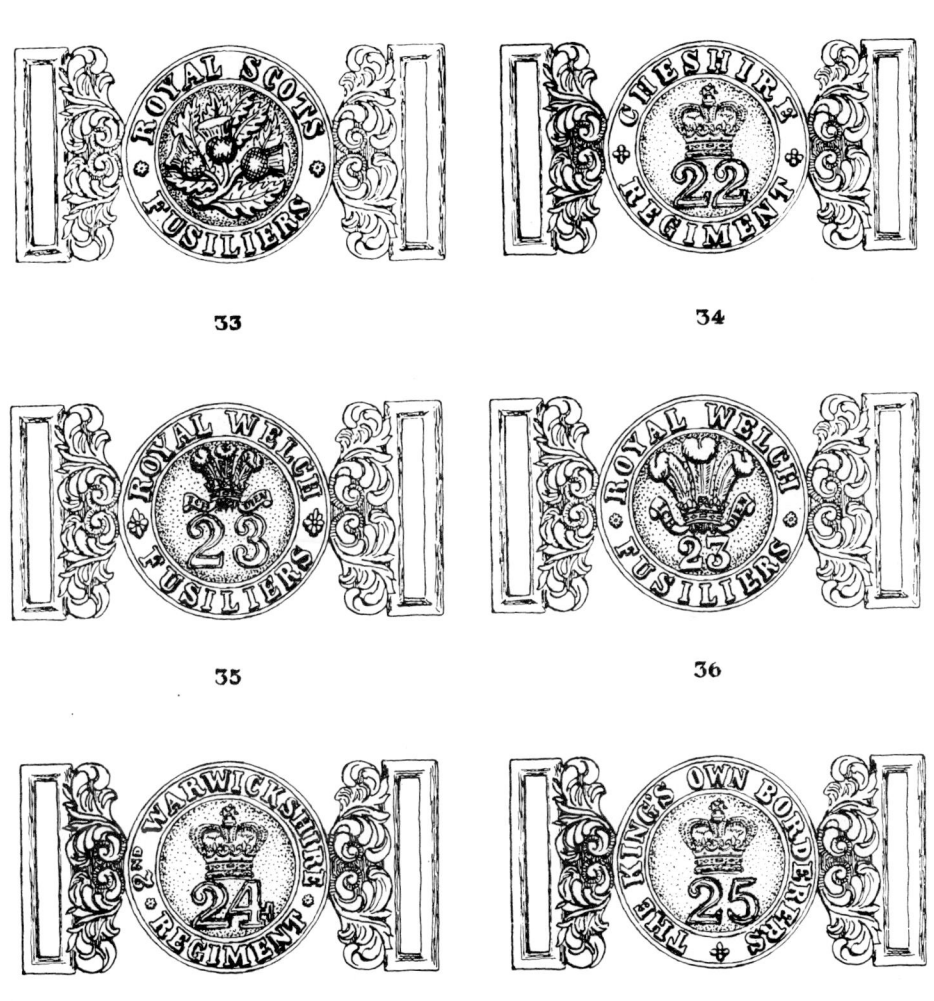

33 34

35 36

37 38

27th Foot. Figure 40, from the Regimental History, is dated 1855 to 1865. It is the standard design, but the concentric pattern of the matt background to the centre is unusual. Figure 41 is dated 1865 to 1881. It conforms to DR 1864 and 1874. Figure 42 is a variant of Figure 41; the main difference is the ground below the Castle.

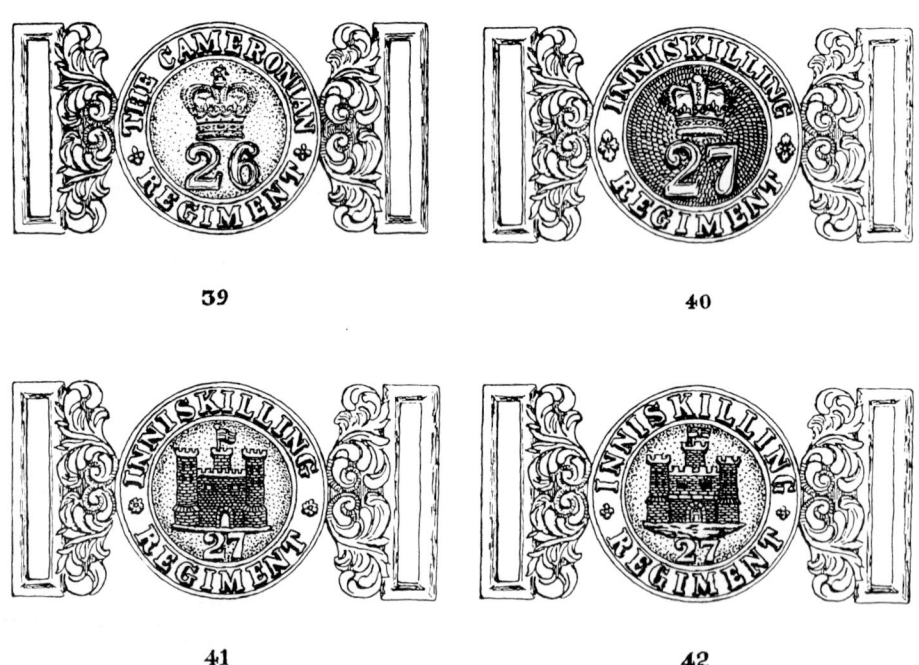

39 40

41 42

28th Foot (Figure 43) and **29th Foot** (Figure 44). Both conform to DR 1855, and I have no evidence of a change before 1881.

30th Foot. Both of these clasps, Figures 45 and 46, match DR 1855 and were worn until 1881. They differ only in the 3.

31st Foot. Figure 47 is another standard pattern. It matches DR 1855 and was doubtless worn until 1881.

32nd Foot. The 32nd did not become light infantry until 1858. Figure 48 therefore must date from 1855 to 1858. Figure 49 was probably worn briefly and supplanted by 50 and/or 51, which were worn until 1881.

33rd Foot. Both Figure 52 and Figure 53 comply with DR 1855. I have no evidence of a change before 1881.

34th Foot. Figure 54 and Figure 55 are as laid down in DR 1855 and were worn until 1881. They differ in the numbers and the definite article in the title.

35th Foot. Figure 56 complies with DR 1855, but Figure 57 is a strange design. It appeared in a Wallis and Wallis sale and was apparently bought by the Regimental Museum. But the complete wreath is unusual and suggests that it may be an Indian Army clasp — Bengal or Madras?

36th Foot. Two more clasps that match DR 1855 and differ only in the numbers (Figures 58 and 59).

37th Foot. Another standard crown-over-number clasp worn until 1881 (Figure 60).

38th Foot. Figure 61 is based on Colonel Cook's article in the *The Bulletin*. He says both the 38th and the 80th had a crown over the Stafford Knot (no number). DR 1864 and 1874 both specify the crown and Knot for the 80th, but not the 38th.

39th Foot. Both Figure 62 and Figure 63 comply with DR 1855. The only difference is the shape of the numbers. Both were probably worn until 1881.

51   52

53

54

55

56

57

58

59

60

61

62

13

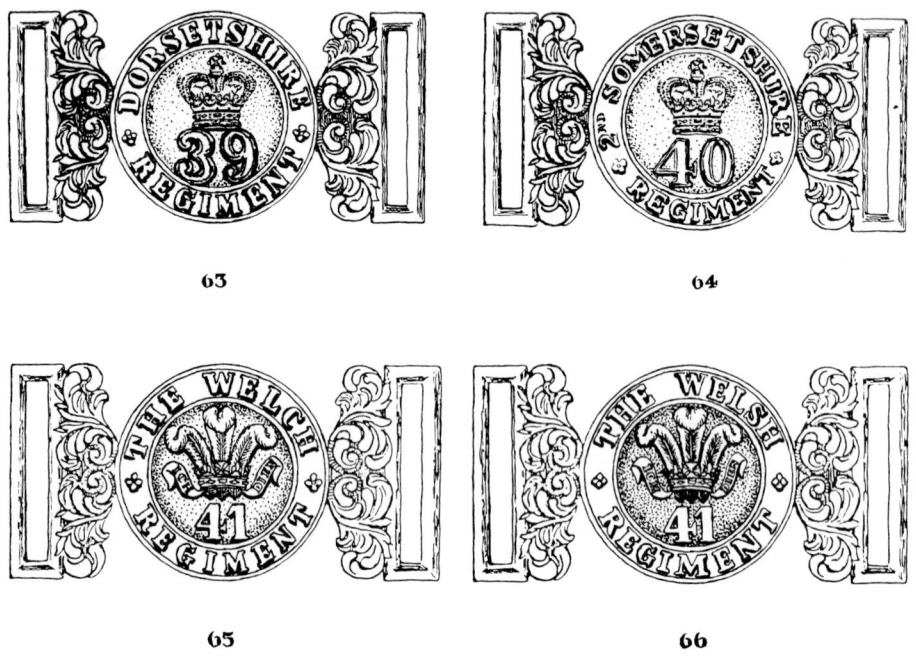

63 64

65 66

40th Foot. Figure 64 conforms to DR 1855, and I know of no change before 1881.

41st Foot. Figures 65 and 66 differ only in the spelling of Welch — Welsh. Figure 65 was worn from 1855 to 1862 and Figure 66 from 1862 to 1881. Both comply with Dress Regulations.

43rd Light Infantry. Figure 67 follows DR 1855. Figures 68 and 69 do also, except for the addition of a crown. Figure 70 was noted in the Regimental Museum, but the lack of the number is strange. This may be a put-together clasp with a centre from a post-1881 clasp and the title from a pre-1881 clasp.

44th Foot. Figure 71 is the standard crown-over-number pattern and conforms to DR 1855. I believe it was worn until 1881 without change.

45th Foot. Figure 72 is also the standard pattern. The 45th's title changed from Nottinghamshire to Nottinghamshire Sherwood Foresters in 1866, but this is too long to get on the title circle, and I have never seen such a clasp.

46th Foot. Figures 73 and 74 differ only in the title circle. South Devonshire would seem more correct, but both basically conform to DR 1855 and were worn until 1881.

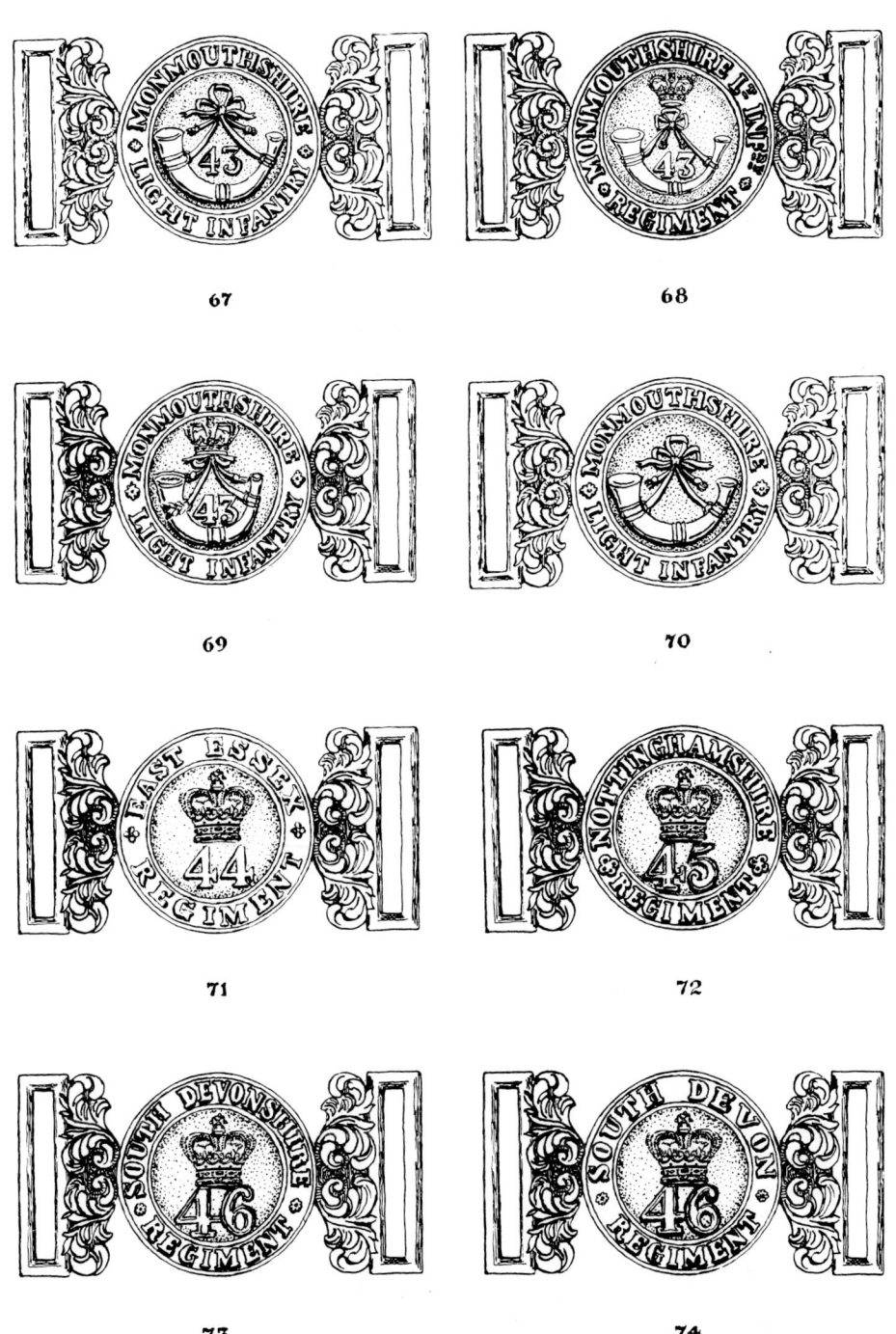

47th Foot. Both Figures 75 and 76 are in the Gaunt Collection, but there is additional evidence of Figure 75. Both match DR 1855, and I believe there were no changes before 1881. It is interesting to note that the 47th's title was The 47th (*The* Lancashire) Regiment of Foot.

48th Foot (Figure 77), **49th Foot** (Figure 78), and **50th Foot** (Figure 79) — all wore clasps conforming to DR 1855. I have no evidence of change before 1881.

51st Light Infantry. Figure 80 was worn from 1855 to 1872, I assume from the Gaunt Collection, as notes there indicate that Figure 81 was worn from 1872 to 1881. Figure 82 is a variant of Figure 81. Figure 83 is an unusual clasp. The centre and the title circle vary slightly from Figures 81 and 82 but the ends are quite different. They resemble the ends on the gold-lace belt for "state occasions and balls" (see Figure 162). The owner describes this clasp as being silver with a gilt wash, rather than the usual plated clasp. It is possible that this clasp was one the Regiment substituted for the standard clasp on the gold-lace belt. None of the applicable Dress Regulations mention a crown for any of these clasps.

52nd Light Infantry. Both Figures 84 and 85, though they look quite different, comply with DR 1855, except for the crown, and were worn, I believe, until 1881.

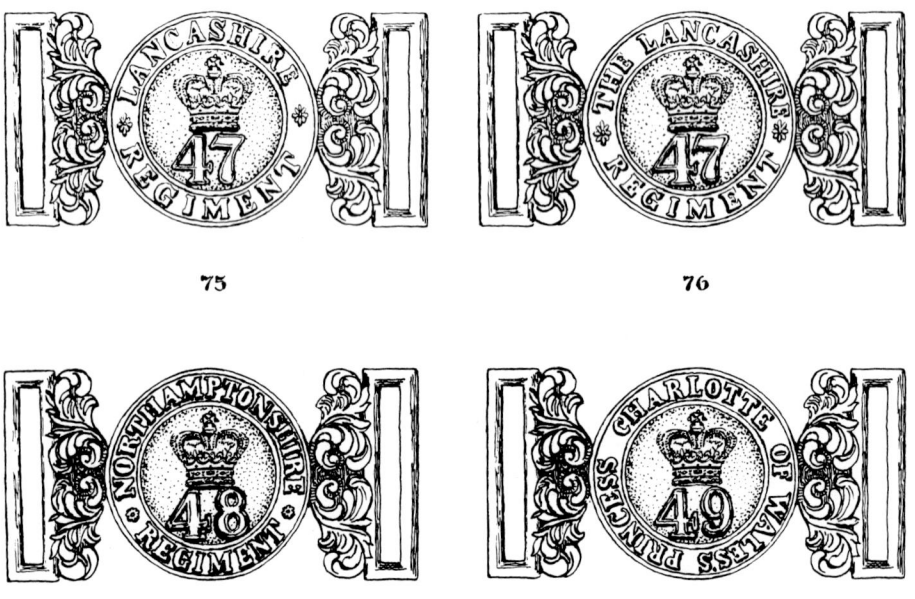

75

76

77

78

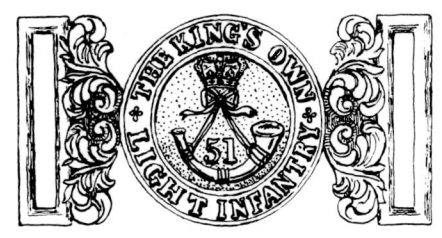

79   80

81   82

83   84

85   86

53rd Foot (Figure 86), **54th Foot** (Figure 87), **55th Foot** (Figure 88), **56th Foot** (Figure 89), **57th Foot** (Figure 90), **58th Foot** (Figure 91), and **59th Foot** (Figure 92) — all wore the standard crown-over-number clasp without change until 1881, so far as I know. One might have expected the 54th to adopt its Sphinx, the 55th its China dragon, and the 56th the Castle and Key. But this does not seem to have happened.

61st Foot (Figure 93), **62nd Foot** (Figure 94), and **63rd Foot** (Figure 95) — all of these conform to DR 1855 and doubtless were worn until 1881.

64th Foot. Figure 96 matches DR 1855 and Colonel Cook's article. Figure 97, from the Gaunt Collection, is marked "W. Jones & Co., 28/6/72," which rather implies that it was supplied to the tailor. Dress Regulations do not mention this pattern.

65th Foot. Figure 98 agrees with DR 1855. DR 1874 call for a crown and tiger. No mention is made of the two battle honour scrolls or the number. The crown is the unusual Georgian one favoured by the 65th (Figure 99).

87

88

89

90

18

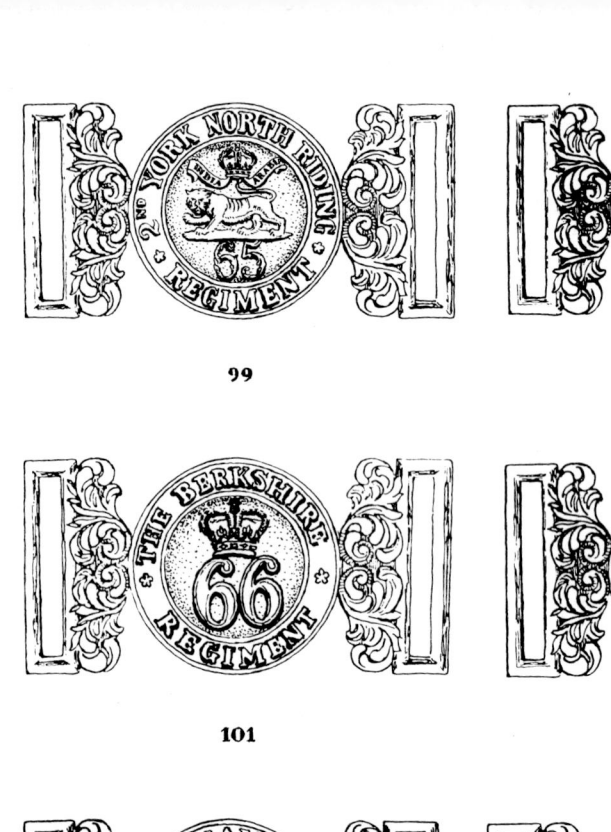

99

100

101 102

103 104

105 106

20

66th Foot. Figures 100 and 101, both from the Gaunt Collection, conform to DR 1855 and were doubtless worn until 1881. The large numbers of Figure 101 are quite unusual.

67th Foot. Figure 102 complies with DR 1855 and was probably worn until 1881.

68th Light Infantry. Figure 103 is from the Gaunt Collection. It may be a prototype that was never actually worn. Figure 104 is drawn from a photograph in a leaflet published by the Regimental Museum.

69th Foot. Figure 105 is another crown-over-number clasp, probably worn until 1881.

70th Foot. Figures 106, 107, and 108 are all variants of the standard clasp, doubtless worn until 1881. Photographs of all three exist. Note that the title of the 70th was The 70th (*The* Surrey) Regiment of Foot. There exists an officers' pattern clasp with differently shaped numbers and a title circle reading SURREY REGIMENT OF FOOT. This is said to be the Regimental Sergeant Major's clasp — obviously very rare.

73rd Foot. Figure 109 is another standard clasp probably worn from 1862 to 1881. The Regiment's title prior to 1862 was just the 73rd Regiment of Foot. There may well have been a crown-over-number clasp, but I do not know what was on the circle — perhaps just REGIMENT and/or a laurel wreath.

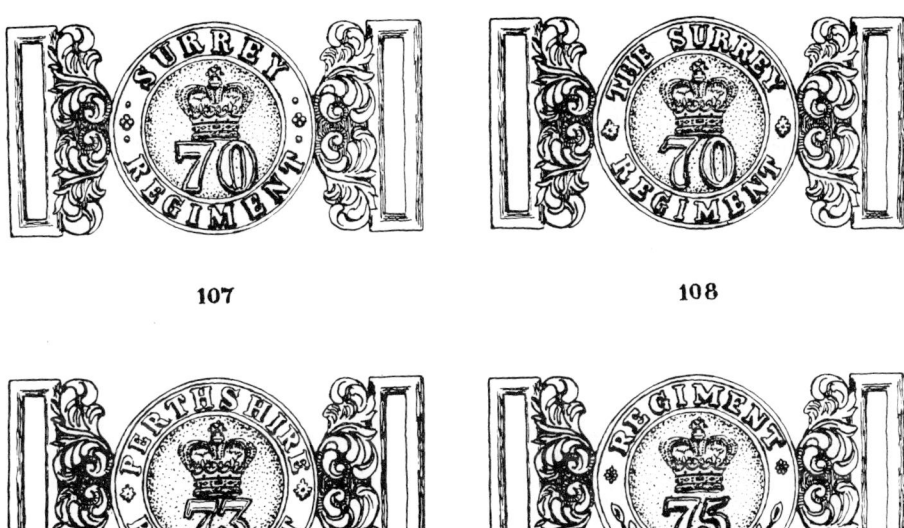

107
108
109
110

111 112

113 114

75th Foot. Figure 110 was worn until the change of title in 1862. There-after Figure 111 was adopted. Dress Regulations do not mention the tiger.

76th Foot. Figure 112 is still another crown-over-number clasp.

77th Foot. Figure 113 is the standard pattern. I do not know when the Regiment changed to Figure 114 — possibly when the title changed in 1876. But the Prince of Wales's plumes really have nothing to do with the title change, and the Regiment did not change the title on the circle. Figures 114 and 115 differ only in the shape of the numbers and were doubtless worn until 1881.

80th Foot. Colonel Cook does not mention Figure 116, but a clasp like this exists and was probably worn from 1855 to 1864. Colonel Cook does show Figure 117, which conforms to DR 1864 and 1874 — except that DR 1864 specify crown and knot above the number.

81st Foot. Figure 118 is the standard pattern and was worn until 1881.

82nd Foot. Figure 119 matches DR 1864 and 1874 and was worn until 1881.

83rd Foot. Figure 120 was worn from 1855 to 1859, when the title changed. Thereafter Figure 121 was worn until 1881.

84th Foot. Figure 122 complies with DR 1864 and 1874 and was worn until 1881.

115   116

117   118

119   120

121   122

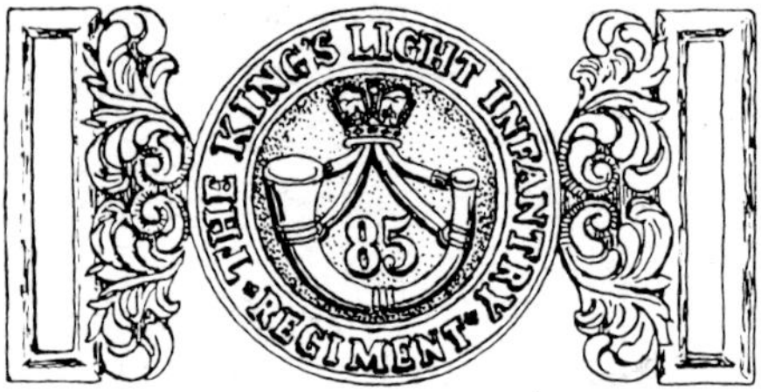

123

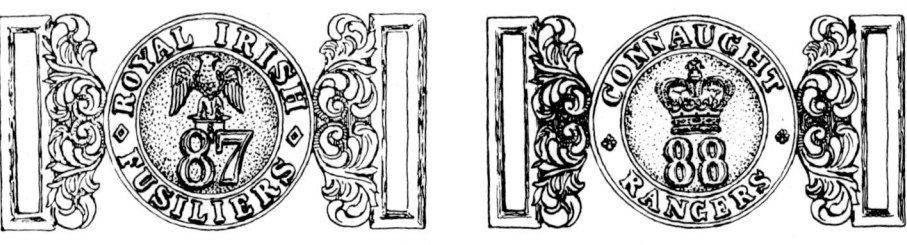

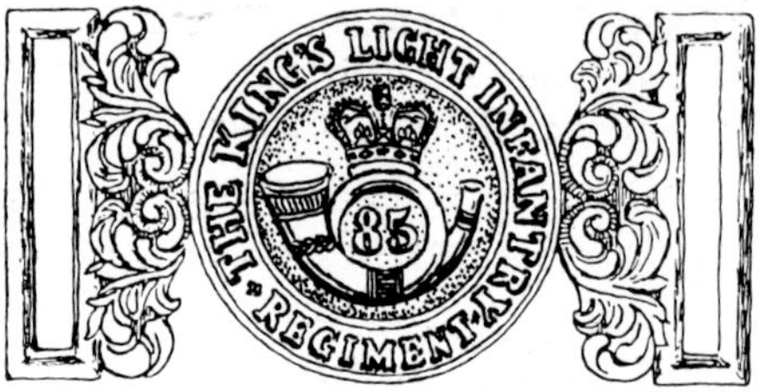

124

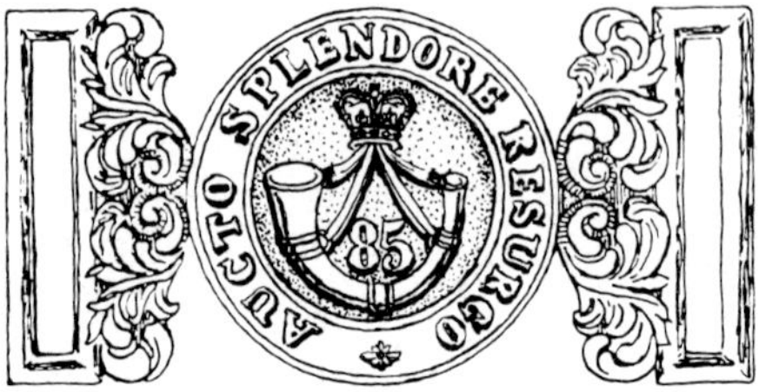

125

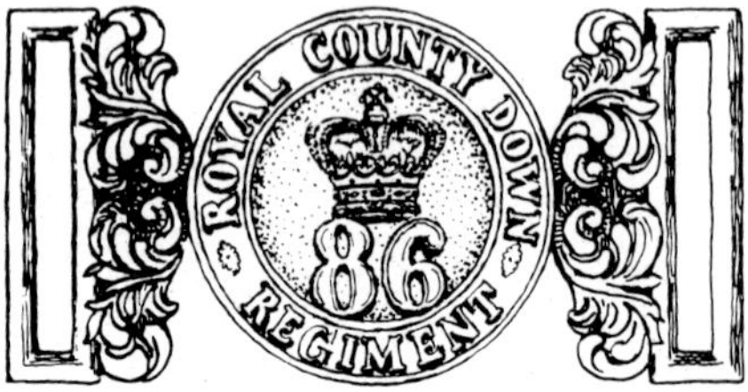

126

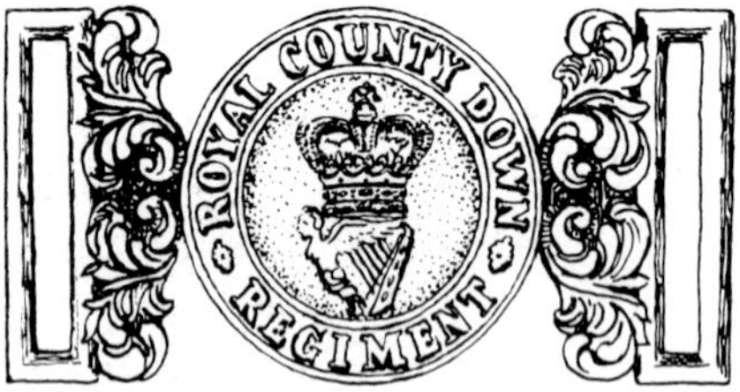

127

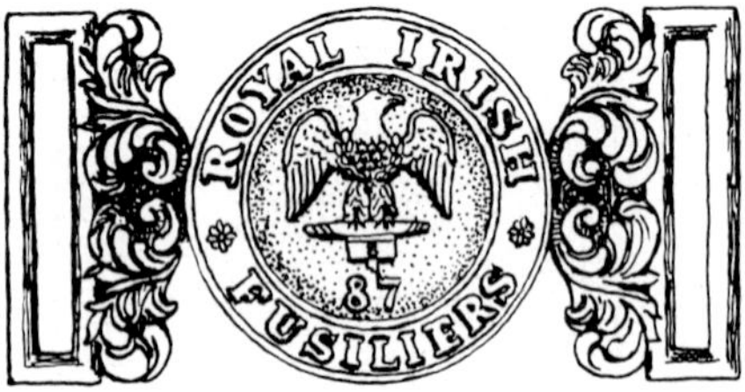

128

129

130

85th Foot. Figures 123 and 124 are the standard pattern except for the crown and were probably worn from 1855 to 1881. Figure 125 is from the Gaunt Collection and may never have been worn.

86th Foot. Figure 126 conforms to DR 1855. Figure 127 is based on the Gaunt Collection, but I have no further confirmation of this clasp.

87th Fusiliers. Figure 128 does not conform to any Dress Regulations. DR 1864 call for a grenade with the Eagle on the ball, and DR 1874 call for a grenade with Eagle and number on the ball. Figure 129 is a variant, with much larger numbers and a smaller Eagle — but still no grenade. One might almost assume the 87th did not wish to be fusiliers!

88th Foot. Figure 130 complies with DR 1855 and was worn until 1881. One might expect a shamrock wreath or a harp and crown, but to my knowledge no such version exists.

89th Foot. Figure 131 conforms to DR 1855. Figure 132 was adopted in 1866 after the change of title. DR 1874 specify Princess Victoria's coronet only, but Figure 133 has the Sphinx and other battle honours — and a Victorian crown. The 89th seems to have ignored Dress Regulations with this clasp. It is noteworthy that the 87th and 89th, later to be linked as The Royal Irish Fusiliers, both displayed a rather cavalier attitude toward Dress Regulations.

90th Foot. Except for the crown, Figure 134 matches DR 1855 and was worn until 1881.

131   132

133   134

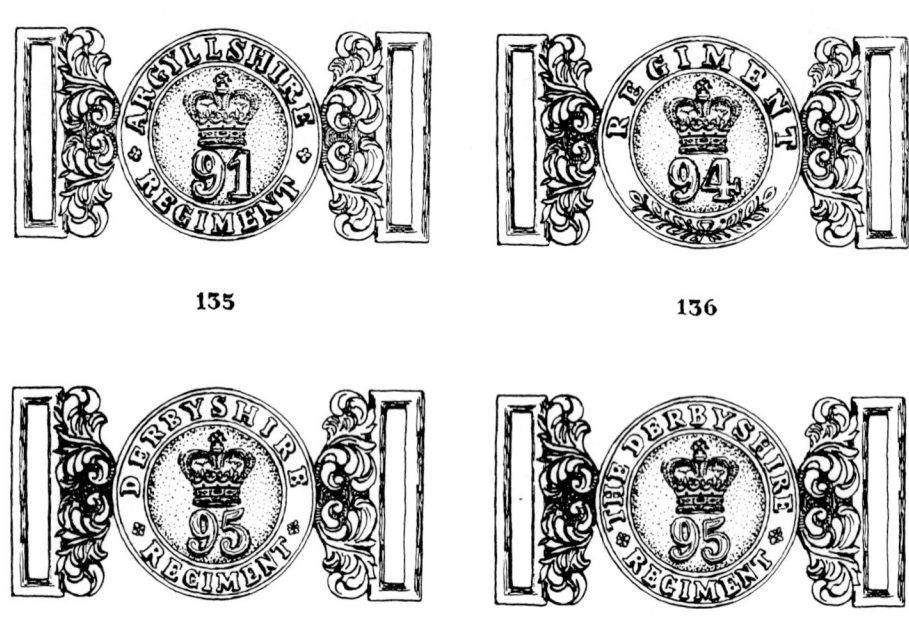

135   136

137   138

91st Foot. Figure 135 complies with DR 1855 and was worn until 1863 when the title changed and the Regiment adopted Highland dress.

94th Foot. Figure 136 is as described in DR 1855 and was worn until 1881.

95th Foot. Both Figures 137 and 138 conform to DR 1855 and were worn until 1881. The 95th's title was The 95th (*The* Derbyshire) Regiment of Foot.

96th Foot. Figure 139 conforms to DR 1855 and was worn until 1881.

97th Foot. Figure 140 comes from the Gaunt Collection and matches DR 1855. Figure 141 is a variant. Both were probably worn until 1881.

98th Foot. Figure 142 complies with DR 1855. In 1876 the title Prince of Wales's was conferred on the Regiment. Figure 143 is based on a photograph that actually lacks the motto scrolls, which were probably broken off. Note that "Own" is not actually a part of the title.

99th Foot. Figure 144 matches DR 1855 and was worn until 1874. When the title changed, the clasp was changed to reflect it (Figure 145).

100th Foot. Figure 146 was worn, I believe, from 1858, when the Regiment was raised, to 1881.

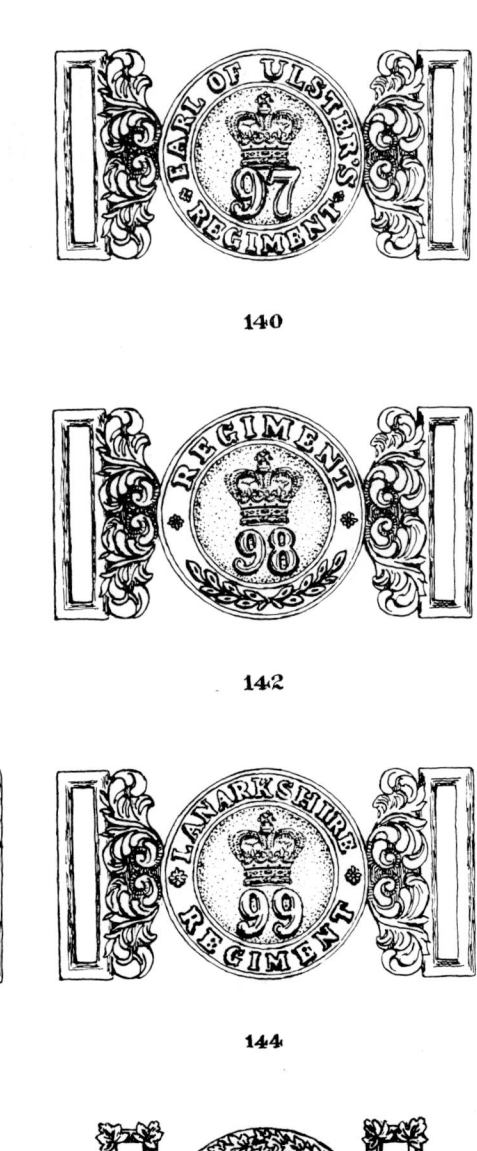

139

140

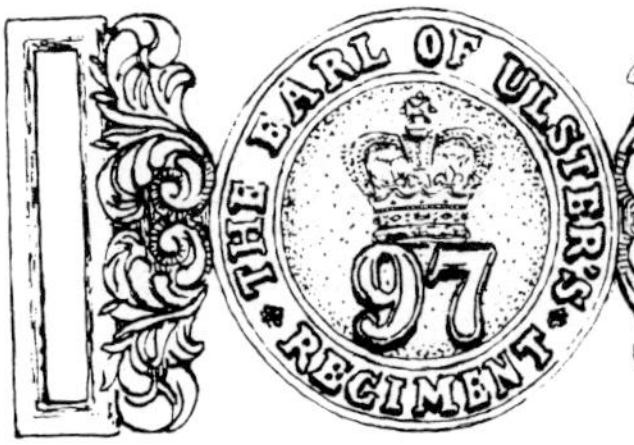

141

142

143

144

145

146

27

The special patterns of the former Honourable East India Company regiments are particularly handsome and display their battle honours and/or mottoes beautifully. The designs of the two light infantry regiments (105th and 106th) are very graceful with their wreaths and horns.

101st Fusiliers. Figure 147 was worn from 1857 to 1861, when Figure 148 was adopted. It was worn until 1881. A colour photograph of 148 seems to show gilt grenade, gilt wreath, gilt battle-honour scrolls, silver crown, strap, and numbers.

102nd Fusiliers. Figure 149 was worn from 1861 to 1881. All of the clasp and mounts are gilt, except for the crown, strap, and numbers, which are silver.

103rd Fusiliers. Figure 150 was worn from 1857 to 1861. In 1861 Figure 151 was adopted and worn until 1881. Again all mounts are gilt, except the crown, strap, and numbers, which are silver. Figure 152 is an interesting variant. It suggests that an officer may have lost the grenade from his waist-belt clasp and substituted a collar badge. Indeed the grenade does not seem to fit well.

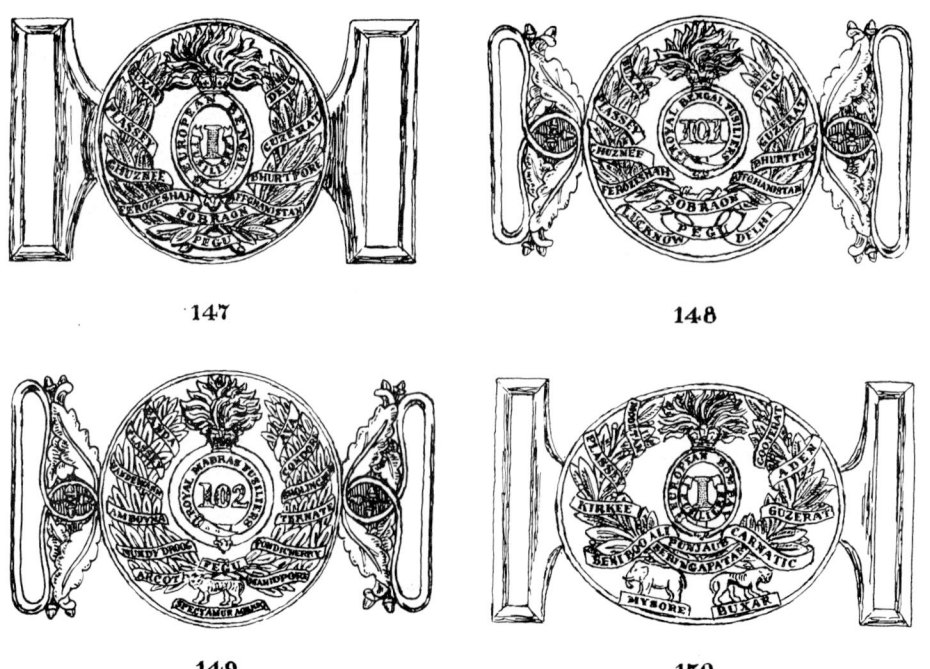

147

148

149

150

151

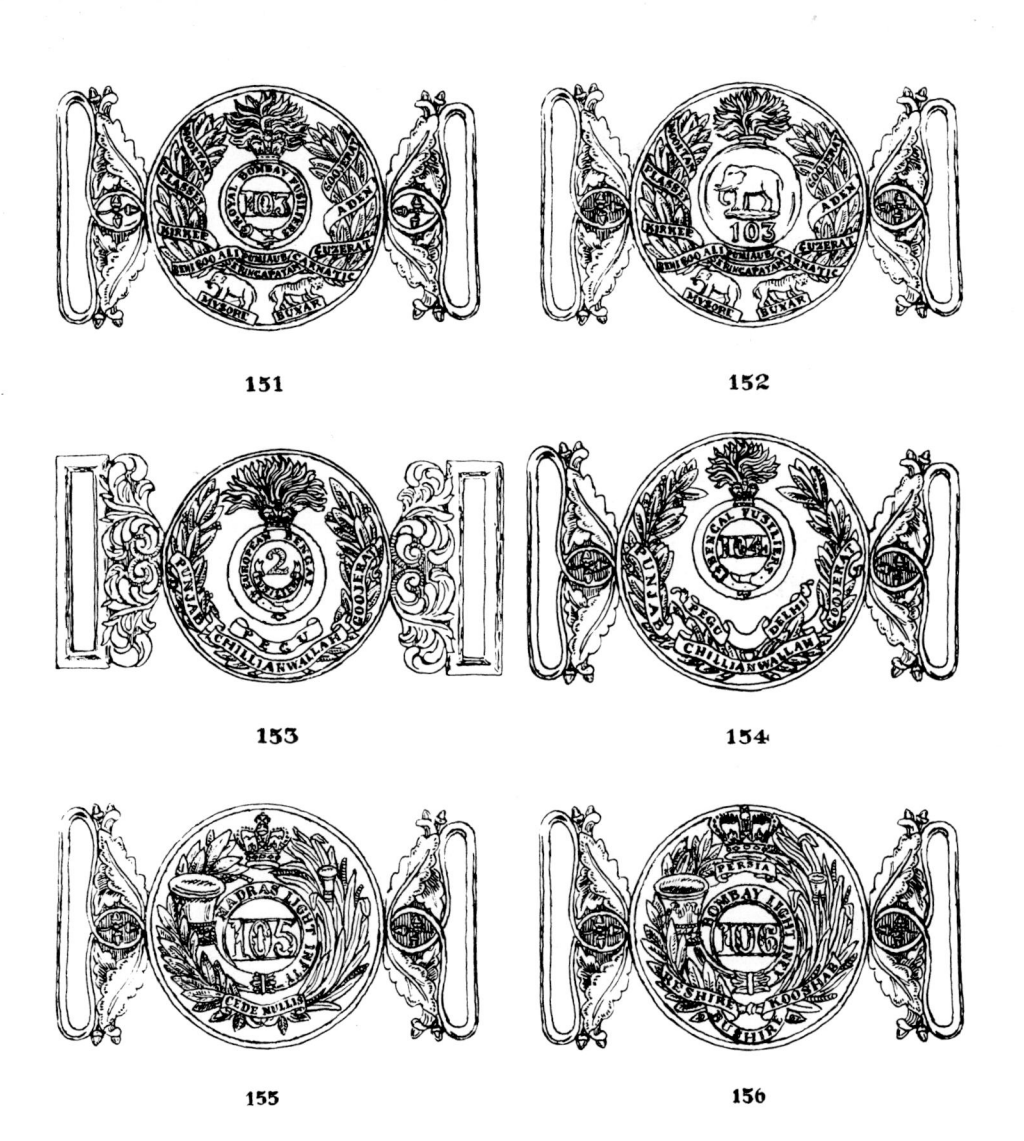

152

153

154

155

156

104th Fusiliers. Figure 153 was worn from 1857 to 1861. In 1861 Figure 154 was taken into use and was worn until 1881. A colour photograph seems to indicate all gilt mounts except the crown, strap, and numbers, which are silver.

105th Light Infantry (Figure 155), **106th Light Infantry** (Figure 156), and **107th Foot** (Figure 157) — all were worn from 1861 to 1881. All the mounts on all three clasps are silver.

29

157

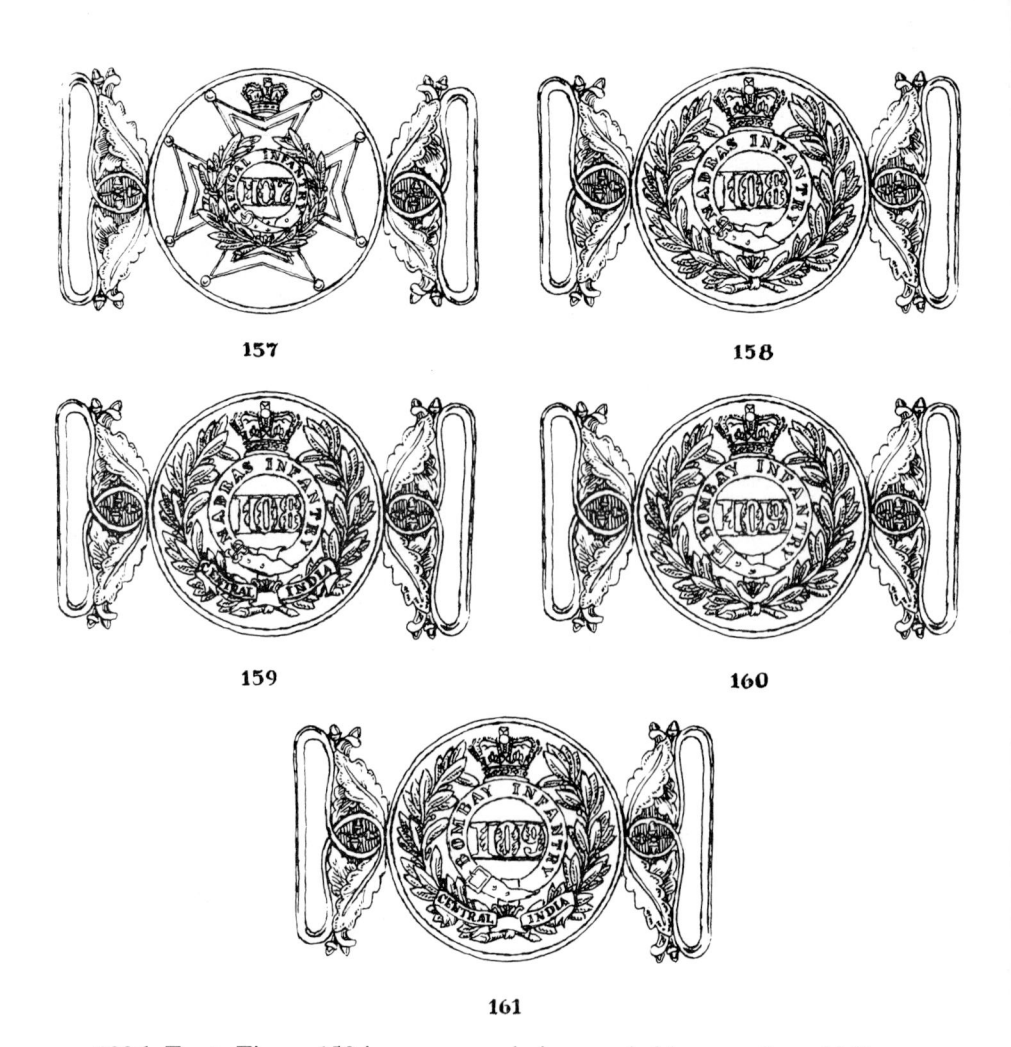

158

159

160

161

108th Foot. Figure 158 is pure speculation, probably worn from 1861 to 1863 when the CENTRAL INDIA honour was granted. Figure 159, which is not speculation, was worn from 1863 to 1881. Careful examination of it indicates that the battle honour scroll was made separately and attached later, giving rise to the speculation that Figure 158 was its predecesor. All mounts are silver. Compare Figures 160 and 161.

109th Foot. Both Figures 160 and 161 are from the Gaunt Collection and were probably worn from 1861 to 1863 and from 1863 to 1881. The metals are the same as those in Figures 158 and 159. The Gaunt rubbings also show a different pattern, possibly worn briefly in 1861 — a fish-roe star with a crowned strap in the centre reading: BOMBAY INFANTRY, 109 in the centre of the strap. It is possible that this was a suggested design only and was never actually worn.

PART II: 1881-1902

The Cardwell Reforms, which took effect in 1881, wrought great changes in the organisation of the British Army. All of the Regular Infantry of the Line regiments lost their old numbers and were given titles. The 110 regiments (including The Rifle Brigade) which had existed prior to 1881 were reduced by amalgamation to 69. County militia units became part of their counties' regular regiments, usually as their 3rd or 3rd and 4th Battalions.

Much as the current "Options For Change" has brought many new badges, so did the Cardwell Reforms, and this extended to waist belt clasps. The basic design of the ends and the title circles showed little change, though more regiments adopted special patterns with acorn ends. But the centres no longer bore the familiar numbers and were filled with regimental badges and battle honours. Several regiments marked their County connections by including one of the militia badges on the new clasps. Some designs had enamelled parts and are quite beautiful.

The King's Royal Rifle Corps and The Rifle Brigade continued to wear their belts under their jackets and the new Royal Irish Rifles (83rd and 86th) joined them. The Cameronians (Scottish Rifles) (26th and 90th) wore an unusual amalgam of rifle and Scottish dress with their own unique waist belt plate.

The 1883 Dress Regulations still give the clasp for The Royal Scots and The King's Own Scottish Borderers. The Royal Scots Fusiliers now wears a rectangular waist belt plate, not clasp, as do the Highland regiments. By the time of the 1891 Dress Regulations, The King's Own Scottish Borderers wears a rectangular plate, but the 1894 Dress Regulations are the first to order a rectangular plate for The Royal Scots.

One or two of the amalgamated regiments that included one or more of the former Honourable East India Company European regiments adopted oak-leaf and acorn ends and large centres — see, for example, The Royal Munster Fusiliers (Figures 238 and 239). Other regiments incorporating a former Honourable East India Company battalion, such as The Royal Sussex Regiment, spurned these more elaborate clasps and stuck to the standard pattern. But a few regiments that had no former Honourable East India Company component opted for the more elaborate clasps and designed their own. One example is The South Staffordshire Regiment, Figure 205.

The 1883 Dress Regulations still refer to an enamelled leather belt. But DR 1891 call for a white buff belt. There is a footnote that reads: "Enamelled leather sword-belts in possession may continue to be worn until they require to be replaced".

The gold-lace belt for state occasions and balls is now more fully described. It was the same for all Infantry of the Line except Scottish and rifle regiments and is shown in Figure 162. This example is gold lace on red morocco leather with a red train; gilt ends and circle to the clasp, silver Royal Crest mounted on a gilt centre.

162

Army Order 39/1902 (issued 1 February 1902) abolished the dress sword belt, ordering in its place a red silk sash. The sword belt was to be a web belt worn under the tunic, with slings for the sword. Therefore the line infantry waist belt clasp as we know it disappeared. The change was not made so quickly that the alteration of crowns was avoided after the death of Queen Victoria on 22 January 1901. There are in existence clasps, the design of which included a crown, that now bear the familiar king's crown instead of Queen Victoria's Crown. But these must have been very short-lived.

In any event, this was the end of waist belt clasps for the Infantry of the Line. They were graceful, often elegant, additions to uniforms — a far cry from the glassy glare of the anodised aluminium waist belt plates one sometimes sees these days.

In all instances below, the examples given conform to all applicable Dress Regulations (1883, 1891, 1894, and 1900), except as specifically noted; and again the badges are silver mounted on gilt centres unless noted otherwise.

The Royal Scots (Lothian Regiment). DR 1883 and 1891 call for the same clasp as Figure 4. Neither 1883 nor 1891 mention The Lothian Regiment for the title circle, though that was part of the title until 1920. The clasp was changed to a rectangular plate for a dirk belt according to DR 1894.

The Queen's (Royal West Surrey Regiment). Figure 163 is the same as Figure 6 except that the number has been removed. The motto is now specifically called for on the circle, but there is some evidence that the title circle might have been worn very briefly after 1881 with the post-1881 centre.

The Buffs (East Kent Regiment). Figure 164 is like Figure 7, except that the number is gone and the title on the circle has changed.

The King's Own (Royal Lancaster Regiment) (Figure 165). The Rose of Lancaster, gilt with red enamel, replaces the IV below the lion of Figure 8, and the title has changed.

163

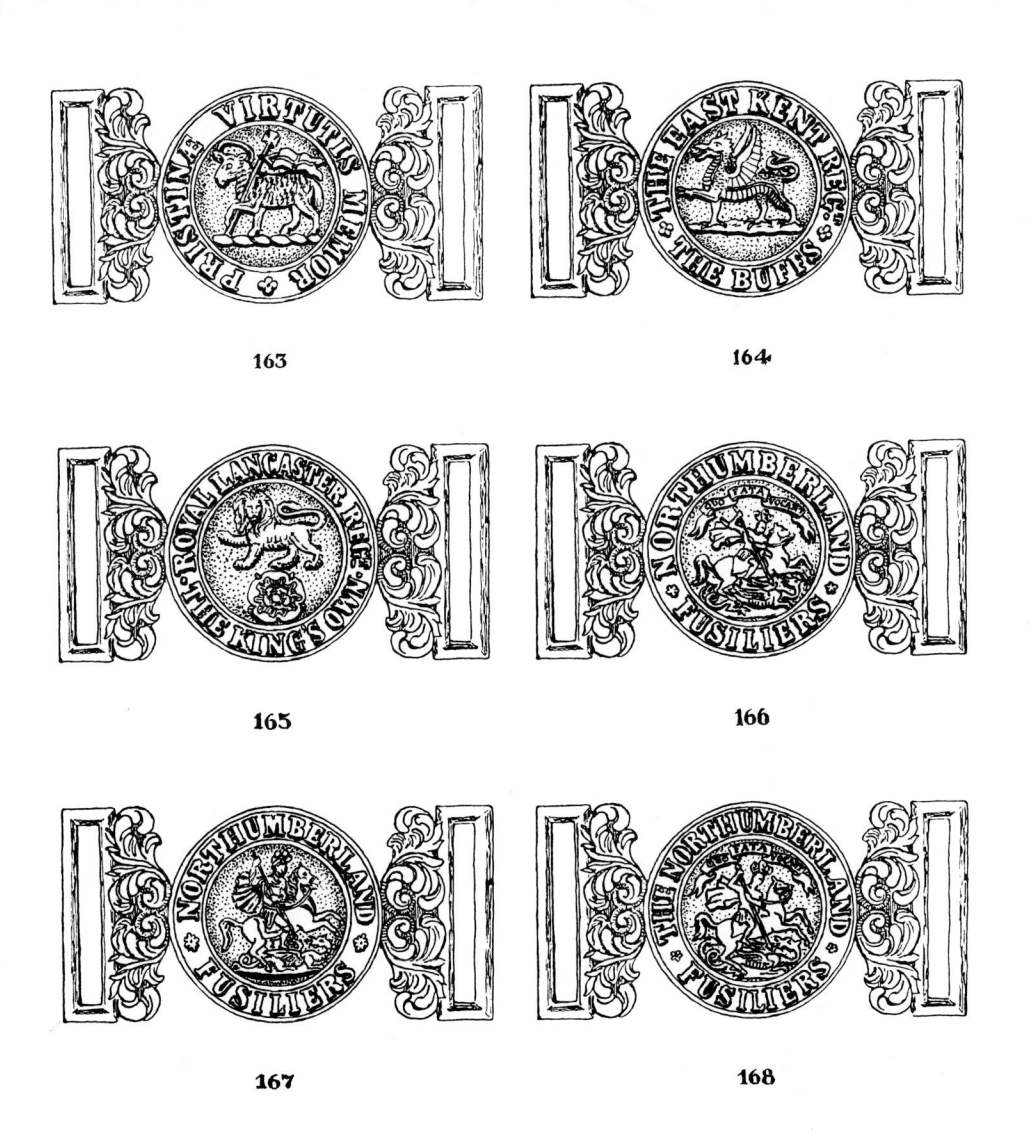

164

165

166

167

168

The Northumberland Fusiliers. Dress Regulations all call for St George and the dragon with motto scroll as Figure 166★. Figure 167, however, lacks the motto. Figure 168 has the motto and the definite article THE.

★ QUO FATA VOCANT — "Whither the Fates call."

33

169 **170**

171 **172**

The Royal Warwickshire Regiment. Figure 169 lacks the number on Figure 12. and the title has changed. Otherwise the two clasps are very similar. On 169 the Antelope and the torse are silver, but the coronet and chain are gilt.

The Royal Fusiliers (City of London Regiment). The rose has lost the number; otherwise Figure 170 is the same as Figure 13. Figure 171 could have been worn only briefly.

The King's (Liverpool Regiment). Figure 172 again is similar to Figure 15 — it has lost the 8 and the title has changed. However, the photograph of an actual clasp on which Figure 172 is based clearly shows plain sans-serif letters for the motto scroll, but all Dress Regulations specify old English letters.

The Norfolk Regiment. Figure 173 still shows Britannia, but she is smaller and has lost the lion and of course the number below, and the title has changed as well. Below Britannia is the Castle of Norwich, a County badge used by both the 1st or West Norfolk Militia and the 2nd or East Norfolk Militia (later the 3rd and 4th Battalions, respectively, of The Norfolk Regiment).

The Lincolnshire Regiment. The Sphinx over EGYPT replaces the number 10 and the crown, and the title has changed (Figure 174).

173

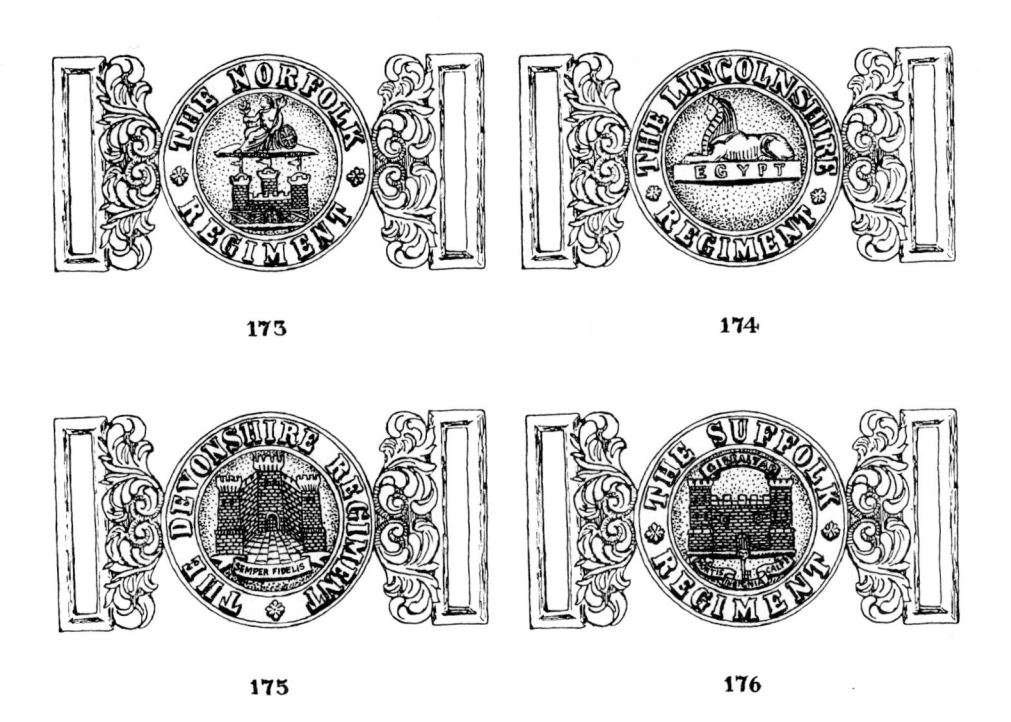

174

175

176

The Devonshire Regiment chose to replace its number with the Castle of Exeter with scroll below inscribed SEMPER FIDELIS★. Figure 175 also shows the new title.

The Suffolk Regiment merely dropped EAST from the title circle of Figure 20 and added THE (Figure 176). My own example of this clasp has a very interesting engraving on the back. It is in German script, a language and a literature with which I am not familiar. It has been translated for me as: "Every life has its own Easter morning. April 4, 1895." That *was* the date of Easter in 1895. The quotation and its applicability to an officer's waist belt clasp of the Suffolk Regiment remain a mystery to me — one of the odd things one runs into in collecting. In 1900 the War Office directed that henceforth the Castle of Gibraltar was to be shown with three towers. However, I have no record that such a variation of the clasp exists.

The Prince Albert's (Somersetshire Light Infantry). Figure 177 is much like Figure 21. The XIII has been replaced with the Sphinx over EGYPT, and the title has changed.

The West Yorkshire Regiment (Figure 178) gave up its White Horse and instead used the tiger for its service in India, and of course the title changed.

★ "Always faithful."

177

178

179

180

The East Yorkshire Regiment (Figure 179) chose the star it had worn on its buttons for some years, with the White Rose of York in the centre on black enamel within a laurel wreath. The facings of the Regiment were not black, but the East Yorkshire Regiment was one of the seven regiments to have a black stripe to their lace — they were at Quebec with Wolfe; and I believe the black enamel commemorates that service.

The Bedfordshire Regiment (Figure 180) placed a silver star on its clasp, with a gilt Maltese cross and Garter, and a silver hart and water. The 1900 Dress Regulations specify blue enamel for the water, but earlier Dress Regulations do not mention it. The hart crossing a ford was the badge of the Hertfordshire Militia, which became the 4th Battalion (Militia) of The Bedfordshire Regiment in 1881.

The Leicestershire Regiment (Figure 181) chose to continue using its tiger with the HINDOOSTAN scroll added above. But the crown is now gone, and the number has been replaced by an Irish harp. This was an unusual honour won by the 3rd Battalion (Militia) for service in Ireland when it was the Leicestershire Militia.

The Royal Irish Regiment. The only change in Figure 182 from Figure 28 is the title on the circle, which replaced the motto. Figure 183 is a variant with a larger wreath and a smaller harp and crown. I have no record of a king's crown version being made.

181

182

183

184

185

186

The Princess of Wales's Own (Yorkshire Regiment) chose for its badge (Figure 184) the cypher and Dannebrog of Alexandra, Princess of Wales. The Regiment was granted the title of Princess of Wales's Own in 1875, and this date appears on the cross. The cross is silver, but the coronet and cypher are gilt. In 1902, according to Brigadier Collins, the design of the cypher changed. Figure 185, he says, was worn by only one or two officers. Indeed, the time element makes it very unlikely that the clasp was worn by many — or for any appreciable length of time.

The Lancashire Fusiliers (Figure 186) combined its Sphinx over EGYPT with a laurel wreath for a simple but graceful design.

The Cheshire Regiment placed on its clasp a silver star with silver Prince of Wales's plumes on a silver ground in the centre within a gilt circle. DR 1883, 1891, and 1894 do not mention a gilt coronet, but DR 1900 do. Earl of Chester is one of the Prince of Wales's titles, hence the plumes (Figure 187).

The Royal Welsh Fusiliers simply dropped the number from its earlier clasp (Figure 36). Dress Regulations do not mention a gilt coronet (Figure 188).

The South Wales Borderers (Figure 189) chose a Welsh dragon within a wreath of laurel rather than immortelles, as one might have expected.

The King's Own Borderers (later, The King's Own Scottish Borderers) changed its crown and number for the Royal Crest (Figure 190). According to the late Mr E. A. Campbell this clasp was worn from 1881 to 1887. Thereafter the Regiment wore a dirk belt and plate. The clasp has indeed disappeared from DR 1891.

The Royal Inniskilling Fusiliers (27th and 108th) adopted a special-pattern clasp, perhaps to commemorate the 2nd Battalion, formerly the 108th (Madras Infantry) Regiment. In both examples shown, the grenade, wreath, and Sphinx over EGYPT are gilt, and the battle honour scrolls, the castle and INNISKILLING scroll, and the horse are silver. But there are some surprising differences between the two clasps. Figure 191 has rococo ends, and Figure 192 has acorn ends. I have a clasp like 191 in my own collection and in addition photographs of such a clasp — four from Wallis & Wallis sales, one from the Regimental History, one from the Durand collection, one from a dealer. But I have only one photograph of 192 with acorn ends. This would seem to indicate that 192 was worn only for a brief period, possibly in the early days after 1881. A further difference is that in 191 the ground below the horse is gilt as is the motto scroll, which conforms to all Dress Regulations. In 192 these are silver. And, last, the honour PYRENEES is misspelled PYRANEES on 192. Curiouser and curiouser . . .

The Gloucestershire Regiment (28th and 61st) placed a Sphinx over EGYPT on its clasp (Figure 193), a happy choice since both battalions had won the honour.

The Worcestershire Regiment (29th and 36th) chose a clasp (Figure 194) with silver star, gilt tower and scroll FIRM. DR 1883 specify a silver FIRM scroll, but both 194 and 195 have the scroll in gilt. The star was an old badge of the 29th, the tower was a Round Tower of Worcester Castle, and "Firm" was an old motto of the 36th. Major Roger Bennett, the expert on The Worcestershire Regiment, tells me that the gilt tower was backed with blue enamel for a short time after 1881 (as on the officers' helmet plates and glengarry badges). Figure 195 is a variant with a silver tower and a title circle lacking the article THE. Major Bennett makes the interesting suggestion that a canny officer in 1881 purchased only the half

187

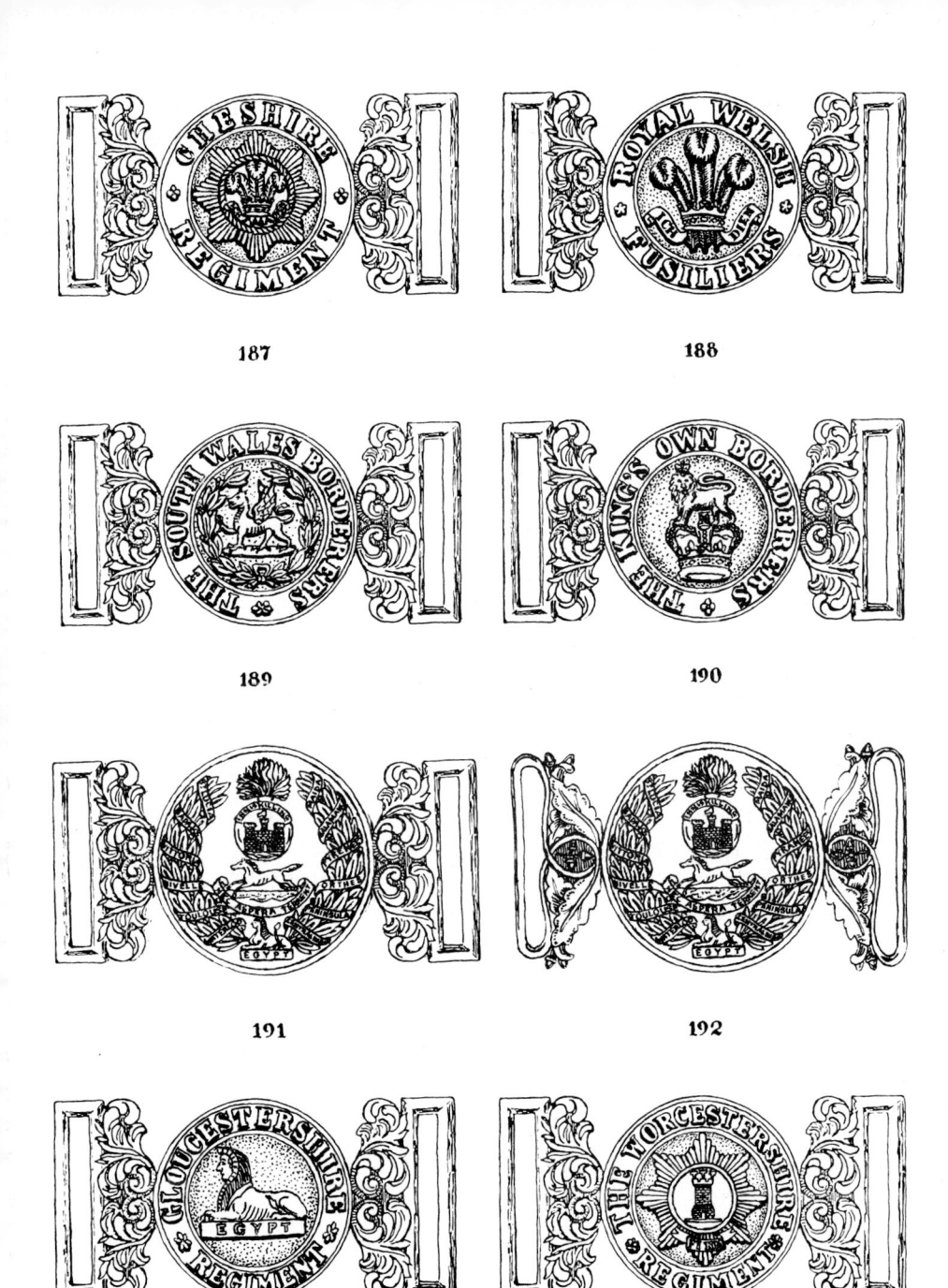

188

189

190

191

192

193

194

39

of the clasp with the centre attached and inserted it into the title circle of his pre-1881 clasp. Canny indeed! Figure 196 was adopted in 1890 to agree with the changes in the helmet plate centre. The star and lion are silver, the Garter and FIRM scroll gilt.

The East Lancashire Regiment (30th and 59th) placed its Sphinx over EGYPT in silver above a gilt rose representing the Rose of Lancaster (Figure 197).

The East Surrey Regiment (31st and 70th) adopted the Arms of Guildford (silver castle and lion on a gilt shield) on a silver star (Figure 198). The Arms were an old badge of the 1st Royal Surrey Militia (later the 3rd Battalion), and the star was a badge of the 3rd Royal Surrey Militia (later the 4th Battalion).

The Duke of Cornwall's Light Infantry (32nd and 46th) placed a ducal coronet above a stringed bugle (Figure 199). The surprise about this one is the acorn ends. I know of only two other regiments — The Welsh Regiment and The Royal Berkshire Regiment — that used acorn ends with the standard pattern of centre and title circle. (See Figures 208, 215, and 216.)

The Duke of Wellington's (West Riding Regiment) (33rd and 76th) adopted the elephant earned by the 2nd Battalion for service in India; this is complete with howdah and caparison (Figure 200).

The Border Regiment (34th and 55th) placed the Garter Star on its clasp, with red enamel in the Cross and blue enamel behind the voided Garter motto (Figure 201). The Garter Star was a badge of the Royal Westmoreland Light Infantry Militia, later 4th Battalion The Border Regiment. All Dress Regulations specify a gilt Garter and motto, but mine is silver.

The Royal Sussex Regiment (35th and 107th) used an interesting combination on its clasp (Figure 202). In the centre are the Garter with motto in silver on blue enamel and the Cross in red enamel on silver. Around the Garter is a laurel wreath of silver with green enamel. This is set on a gilt Maltese cross, which in turn rests on a silver Roussillon plume. DR 1883, 1891, and 1894 are not clear about the Garter and motto, but I believe this is what is meant, and DR 1900 spell it out. The Garter Star was an old badge of the Royal Sussex Light Infantry Militia, later 3rd Battalion The Royal Sussex Regiment. The Maltese cross is said to commemorate the capture of Malta in 1800, but I believe its use on the clasp also refers to the Regiment's 2nd Battalion, the 107th (Bengal Infantry) Regiment, which used a Maltese cross on its badges (see Figure 157). The Roussillon plume is said to have been won from the French regiment of that name at Quebec★.

★ For an interesting discussion of this plume, see *The Bulletin* (The Military Historical Society), No. 147, p. 116; No. 149, pp. 45-46; No. 150, pp. 101-103; No. 152, pp. 176-178.

195

196

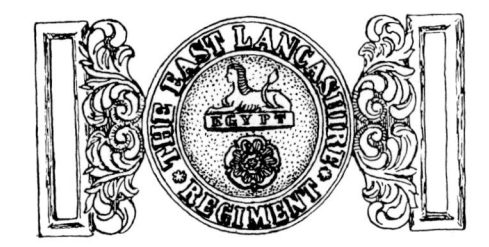

197

198

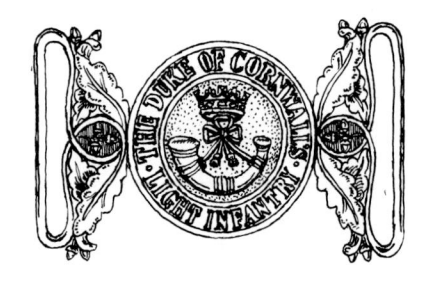

199

200

201

202

41

203

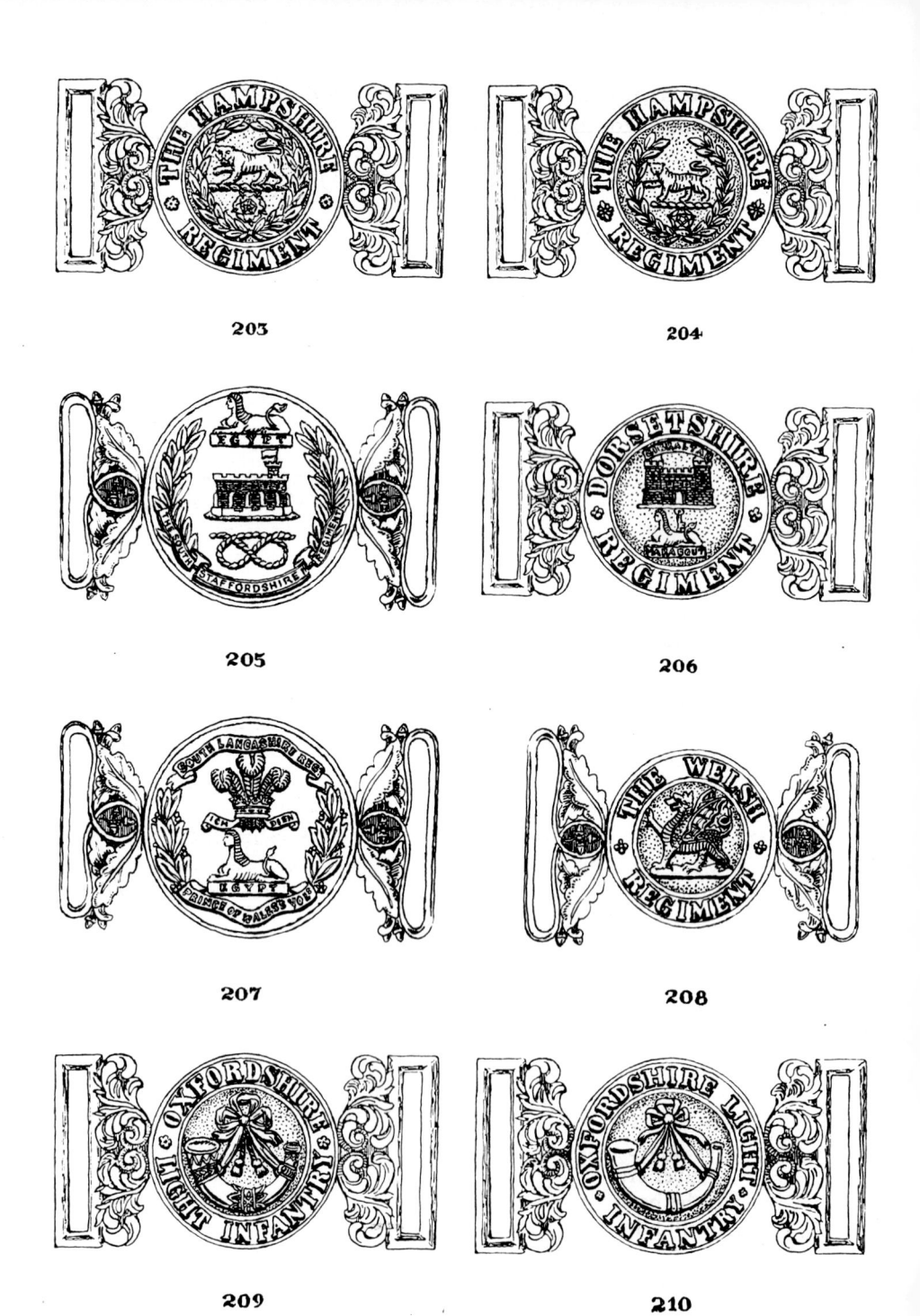

204

205

206

207

208

209

210

42

The Hampshire Regiment (37th and 67th) placed on the centre of its clasp a silver tiger, for the 67th's service in India, on a torse above a gilt rose with red and green enamel, all within a silver laurel wreath (Figure 203). Figure 204 has a different-sized wreath and tiger, but the main elements remain the same. The rose is said to have been given to the County by Henry V. It was an old badge of the Hampshire Militia, which became 3rd Battalion The Hampshire Regiment.

The South Staffordshire Regiment (38th and 80th) adopted a special pattern clasp with acorn ends, all mounts being in silver (Figure 205). The Castle in the centre is the Round Tower of Windsor Castle, an old badge of (The King's Own) 1st Staffordshire Militia, later 3rd Battalion The South Staffordshire Regiment.

The Dorsetshire Regiment (39th and 54th) combined the Castle and Key and GIBRALTAR of the 39th with the Sphinx over MARABOUT of the 54th below (Figure 206).

The Prince of Wales's Volunteers (South Lancashire Regiment) (40th and 82nd) adopted a special pattern clasp, with acorn ends, on which it displayed the Prince of Wales's plumes (all silver including the coronet) for the 82nd and the Sphinx over EGYPT for the 40th. There exists a crudely cast version of this clasp, of a silvery metal — very much a "bazaar-made" item. Major J. Kenny, then Curator of the Regimental Museum, told me that warrant officers and senior non-commissioned officers wore these in walking-out dress in India.

The Welsh Regiment (41st and 69th) took the Welsh dragon, an old badge of the Royal Glamorganshire Light Infantry, with acorn ends, which are unusual with the normal centre and title circle (Figure 208). The Royal Glamorganshire Light Infantry became 3rd Battalion The Welsh Regiment in 1881.

The Oxfordshire Light Infantry (43rd and 52nd) naturally continued its light infantry bugle. The main difference between Figures 209 and 210 is the arrangement of the title on the circle.

The Essex Regiment (44th and 56th) adopted a special pattern clasp with acorn ends (Figure 211). There is a large silver oak wreath around a title circle with silver crown above. The shield in the centre bears the Arms of Essex, and the background of the shield is red enamel on gilt. The inset seaxes have gilt hilts and silver blades. The silver Castle and Key below are the Gibraltar honours of the 56th, and the silver Sphinx over EGYPT above is an honour of the 44th. Altogether a handsome clasp. I know of no king's crown version.

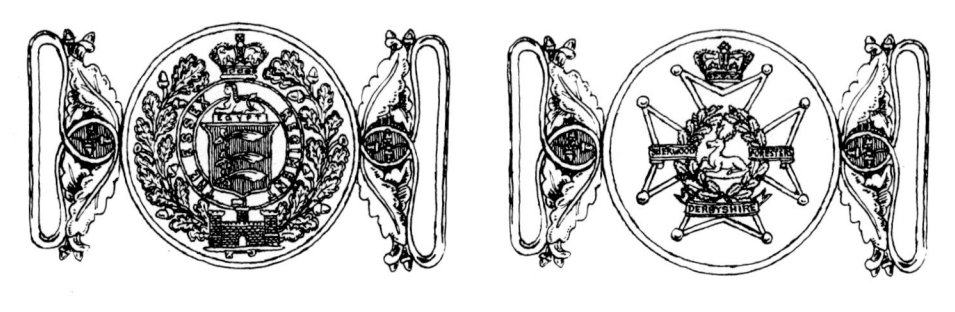

211   212

The Sherwood Foresters (Derbyshire Regiment) (45th and 95th) also introduced a special pattern clasp with acorn ends (Figure 212). The crown and Maltese cross are silver; the wreath, SHERWOOD FORESTERS scrolls, and DERBYSHIRE scroll are gilt; the hart is silver on a blue enamel background. The hart is a badge derived from the Arms of Derby. There are minor differences in the shape of the cross and the crown, but I know of no king's crown version. Another handsome clasp.

The Loyal North Lancashire Regiment (47th and 81st) took the Royal Crest in silver above a gilt rose, the Red Rose of Lancaster, with red and green enamel (Figure 213). The Royal Crest was also the crest of the Duchy of Lancaster. Again I do not know of a king's crown version.

The Northamptonshire Regiment (48th and 58th) took the Castle and Key with scroll GIBRALTAR above (for the 58th) and TALAVERA below (for the 48th) (Figure 214). I do not know of a three-tower version.

Princess Charlotte of Wales's (Berkshire Regiment) (49th and 66th) displayed the China dragon of the 49th in the centre of a clasp with acorn ends (Figure 215). After 1885, when the Regiment was accorded the honour of being made a Royal regiment, the title became Princess Charlotte of Wales's (Royal Berkshire Regiment), and the circle was changed to conform (Figure 216).

The Queen's Own (Royal West Kent Regiment) (50th and 97th) used the Royal Crest, an old badge of the 50th (Figure 217). Again I do not know of a king's crown version.

The King's Own Light Infantry (South Yorkshire Regiment) (51st and 105th). Figure 218 conforms to DR 1883, though the title isn't specified. The title shown is the same as the 51st's prior to 1881. The bugle is gilt, according to DR 1883, but all subsequent Dress Regulations show it as silver. However, the specimen seen has both the crown and the bugle in gilt, with the rose and motto scroll in silver. DR 1883 specify a crown, but not what kind. The Guelphic crown is a surprise. It had been used previously on the officers' shoulder belt plate prior to 1855 but the reason

213

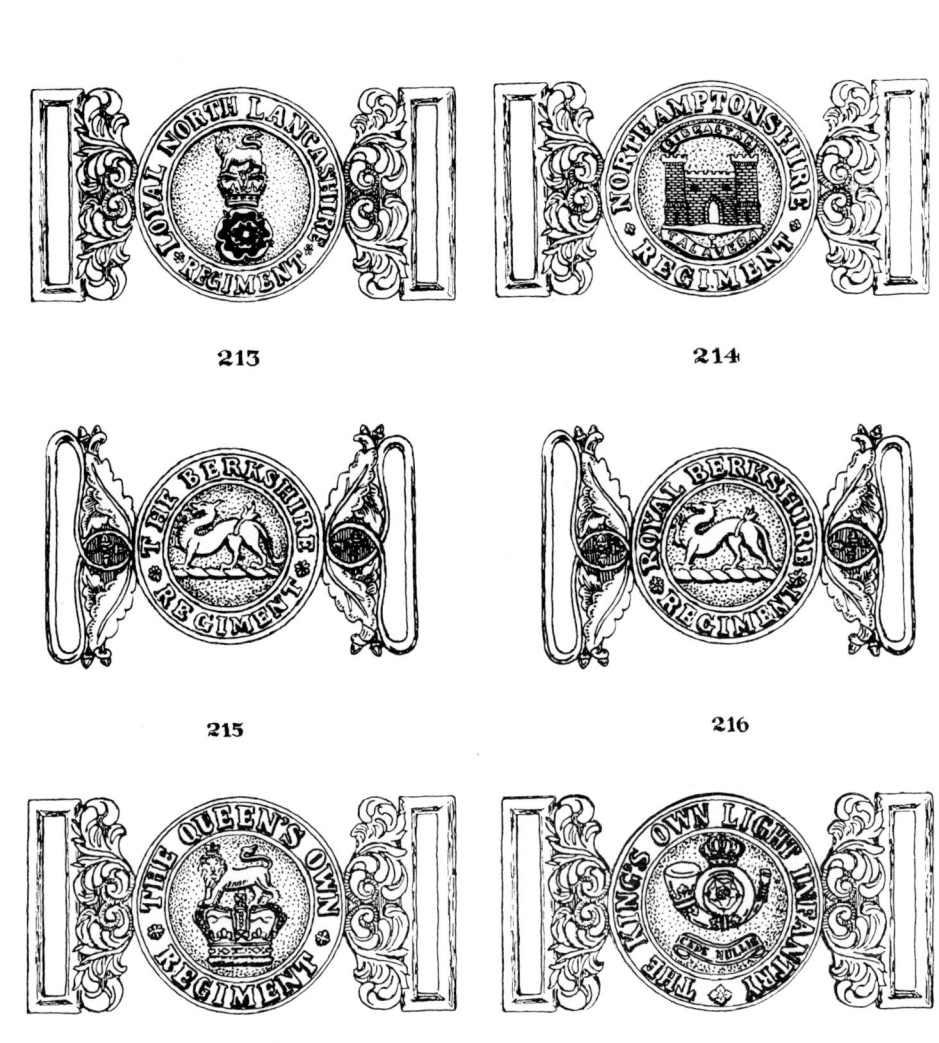

214

215

216

217

218

219

220

221

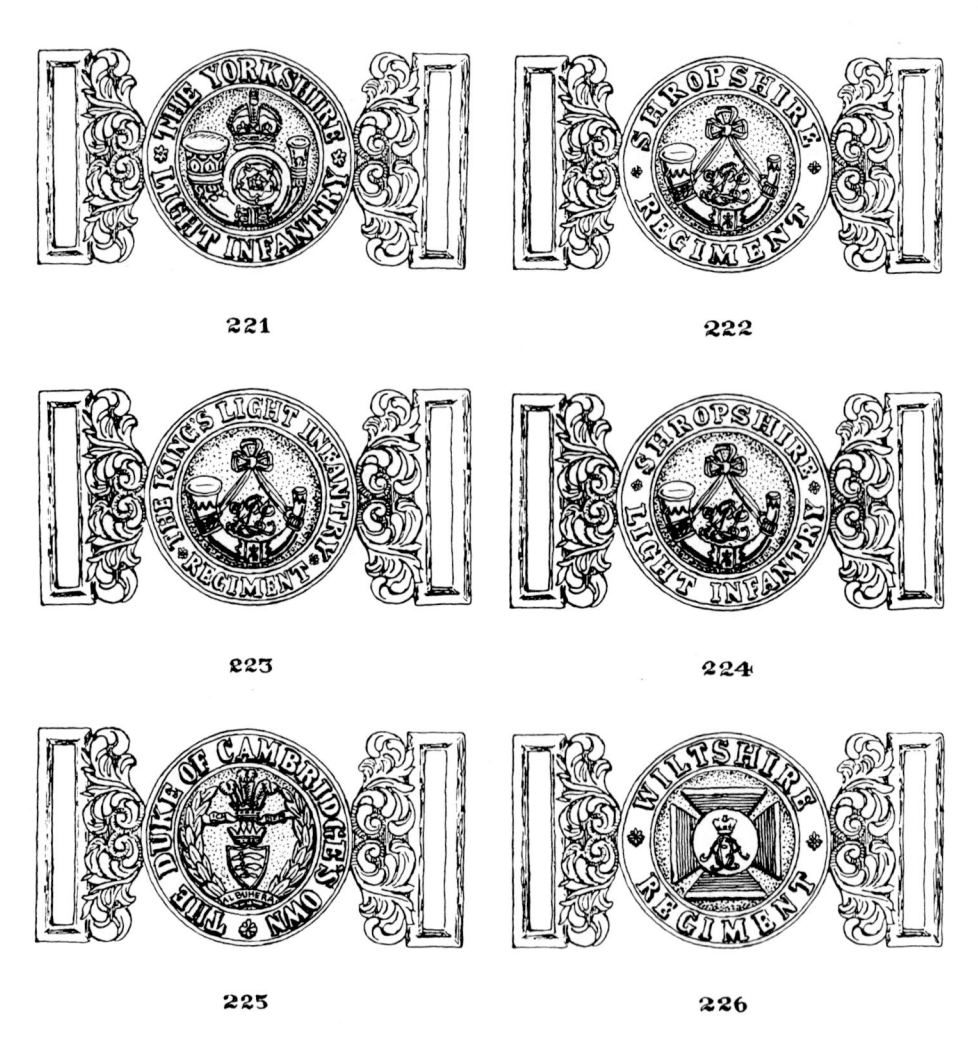

222

223

224

225

226

for reverting to its use after 1881 is unclear. The CEDE NULLIS★ scroll came from the 105th. Figure 219 does not correspond to any Dress Regulations, and I cannot explain the omission of the crown. Figure 220 presumably came into use in 1887, when the title changed from The King's Own Light Infantry (South Yorkshire Regiment) to The King's Own (Yorkshire Light Infantry). This complies with DR 1891, 1894, and 1900. Figure 221, with a king's crown, could have been worn only briefly.

The King's (Shropshire Light Infantry) (53rd and 85th). The cypher KLI is gilt. Figure 222 was probably worn only from 1881 to 1882 and possibly by the 1st Battalion only, since the title comes from its title prior to 1881. Figure 223 again was worn from 1881 to 1882, this time possibly

★ "Yield to none."

by the 2nd Battalion only, since the title echoes its title prior to 1881. Figure 224 was adopted in 1882 and agrees with all Dress Regulations.

The Duke of Cambridge's Own (Middlesex Regiment) (57th and 77th). Figure 225 complies with all Dress Regulations — except that none of them mention the Saxon crown. A pleasing combination of elements from the two previous regiments makes an attractive clasp — the Albuhera wreath and scroll from the 57th, the Prince of Wales's plumes from the 77th, and the Arms of Middlesex, which apply to both.

The Duke of Edinburgh's (Wiltshire Regiment) (62nd and 99th). The Wiltshire Regiment adopted the Maltese cross of the 62nd and the coronet and cypher of the Duke of Edinburgh from the 99th (Figure 226). The cross is gilt, and the coronet and cypher are silver. All Dress Regulations specify the title on the circle as THE WILTSHIRE REGIMENT. But the only photograph of this clasp I have lacks THE.

The Manchester Regiment (63rd and 96th) adopted a clasp that refers only to the 2nd Battalion — the Sphinx over EGYPT had been awarded to an earlier 96th (Figure 227). The star is silver, and the Sphinx over EGYPT is gilt.

The Prince of Wales's (North Staffordshire Regiment) (64th and 98th) took the 98th's Prince of Wales's plumes (Figure 228). There is no Stafford Knot this time.

227   228

229   230

The **York and Lancaster Regiment** (65th and 84th) made a handsome clasp with the silver tiger of the 65th and the Union Rose, gilt and silver, of the 84th (Figure 229). The title is exactly as given in all Dress Regulations. However, a version with the title shown in Figure 230 does exist.

The **Durham Light Infantry** (68th and 106th) adopted a standard light infantry design (Figure 231). Both component regiments had been light infantry and there is no particular reference to either regiment on this clasp.

Princess Victoria's (Royal Irish Fusiliers) (87th and 89th) used special shamrock and harp ends. Figure 232 complies with all Dress Regulations. The title circle has a crown and laurel wreath with the title on three scrolls. And finally the Regiment displays a grenade — with its French Eagle on the ball. The grenade is gilt and the Eagle silver. Figure 233 has quite a different title circle. I have an example of Figure 232 and in my files photographs of several other examples, but I have only one picture of Figure 233. Therefore I feel reasonably confident that 233 was worn very briefly, probably 1881-82.

The Connaught Rangers (88th and 94th) adopted the 2nd Battalion's elephant to commemorate Seringapatam and service in India, which had been won by an earlier 94th (Figure 234). Figure 235 is another clasp that could have been worn only briefly in 1901 or 1902.

The Prince of Wales's Leinster Regiment (Royal Canadians) (100th and 109th) introduced fine special ends with maple leaves (Figure 236) referring to the 100th's Canadian origins. The special pattern centre has a wreath of combined laurel and maple leaves. A crowned title circle surrounds the Prince of Wales's plumes. Figure 237 is the same except for the addition of the battle honour scroll CENTRAL INDIA from the 109th. It is possible that Figure 236 was worn briefly by the 1st Battalion after 1881 or by a militia battalion. DR 1883 call for the battle honour on the clasp. All Dress Regulations specify a gilt scroll for the honour, with the balance of the design silver. DR 1900 stipulate a gilt coronet.

231

232

233

234

235

236

237

238

49

239 **240**

The Royal Munster Fusiliers (101st and 104th) continued with a special pattern with acorn ends. The wreath with battle honour scrolls and a title scroll is all silver. The grenade is gilt with silver tiger (Figure 238). Figure 239 is shown because the grenade is noticeably smaller than that on 238.

The Royal Dublin Fusiliers (102nd and 103rd) also continued with a special pattern but with ends like those of the Royal Irish Fusiliers (Figure 240 — see also Figures 232 and 233). All the mounts are gilt except the title circle and the harp on the grenade, which are silver. The motto SPECTAMUR AGENDO★ came from the 102nd as did the tiger over PLASSEY. The elephant over MYSORE came from the 103rd.

And to end this (for my sake) a ladies' belt clasp, though I have seen it described as a levée dress clasp! It is gilt filigree with a regimental badge mounted in silver on each piece. I have one (Figure 241) that was supposed to be the clasp of a lady whose husband (?) served in the 19th Hussars. Careful examination of the two Dannebrogs, however, shows that one bears the date 1885 and the other 1875, which makes it a Green Howards' badge. This is, no doubt, a manufacturer's error. But I do prefer to think that the lady shared her favours between the 19th Hussars and The Green Howards (19th Foot).

241

★ "We are judged by our actions."

SOURCES

Figure
1. Author's collection.
3. Photograph from Mr R. G. Harris.
4. Collection of the late Admiral W. G. Whiteside, OBE, USN.
5. DR 1864 and 1874.
6. Photograph from Mr R. G. Harris.
7. Wallis & Wallis Sale 169, August 1970*.
8. Photograph from Mr R. G. Harris.
9. Sumner, Percy. *St. George's Gazette*, December, 1900, p.208.
10. DR 1864, 1874.
11. National Army Museum 5910-271-1, "J.R." Book among the archives in the Gaunt Collection.
12. DR 1864, 1874.
13. Collection of Mr John Atkin.
14. W&W 344, 1/90.
15. W&W 169, 8/70.
16. W&W 321, 6/87.
17. Photograph from Mr R. G. Harris.
18. Mr John Atkin's collection.
19. Webb, Lieutenant Colonel E. A. H. *History of the 12th (The Suffolk) Regiment. 1685-1913*. London: Spottiswoode & Co., Ltd., 1914.
20. *Ibid.*
21. National Army Museum 5910-271-1, "J.R." Book among the archives in the Gaunt Collection.
22. *Ibid.*
23. Photograph from Mr R. G. Harris.
24. Mr John Atkin's collection.
25. Mr John Atkin's collection.
26. Author's collection.
27. Webb, Lieutenant Colonel E. A. H. *History of the Services of The 17th (The Leicestershire) Regiment*. London: Vacher & Sons Limited, 1911.
28. Admiral Whiteside's collection.
29. Photograph from Mr R. G. Harris.
30. Mr John Atkin's collection.
31. Photograph from Mr R. G. Harris.
32. Photograph from Mr R. G. Harris.
33. Mr Douglas N. Anderson and Mr K. R. A. Gibbs.
34. Mr John Atkin's collection.
35. W&W 169, 8/70.
36. Photograph from Mr R. G. Harris.
37. Photograph from Mr R. G. Harris.
38. Notes made by the late Mr E. A. Campbell.
39. Notes made by the late Mr E. A. Campbell.
40. *Royal Inniskilling Fusiliers, Being the History of the Regiment from December 1688 to July 1914*. Compiled under the Direction of a Regimental Historical Records Committee. London: Constable & Company Ltd., 1928.
41. *Ibid.*
42. The collection of Field Marshal Sir John Chapple, GCB, CBE.
43. W&W 169, 8/70.
44. W&W 169, 8/70.

* Hereinafter cited as W&W, followed by the sale number, month, and year.

Figure
45. Photograph from Mr R. G. Harris.
46. Admiral Whiteside's collection.
47. Sketch from Mr W. Y. Carman, FRHistS, FSA, FSA (Scot).
48. Ivall, D. Endean, and Thomas, Charles. *Military Insignia of Cornwall*. Penwith Books in Association with DCLI Regimental Museum, 1974.
49. *Ibid*.
50. W&W 324, 10/87.
51. Admiral Whiteside's collection.
52. Admiral Whiteside's collection.
53. W&W 309, 2/86.
54. W&W 169, 8/70.
55. "Chaco Plates . Helmet Plates . Breast Plates and Sword Belt Clasps of the 34th (Cumberland) Regiment and 55th (Westmorland) Regiment," Part III, by the Editor. *The Border Magazine*, March 1949, p. 165.
56. Photocopies from the West Sussex Record Office and the Sussex Combined Services Museum.
57. *Ibid*.
58. Pereira, Captain H. P. E. "The Badges of the Worcestershire Regiment." *Firm*, the Regimental Magazine, January 1948. Figure 116.
59. Pereira, Captain H. P. E., *op. cit.*, July 1948. Figure 134.
60. W&W 169, 8/70.
61. Cook, Colonel H. C. B., OBE. "The Staffords and the 'Stafford Knot' ", *The Bulletin*, The Military Historical Society, Vol. XXI, No. 84, May 1971, pp. 105-120.
62. Photograph from Mr R. G. Harris.
63. W&W 369, 10/92.
64. Smythies, Captain R. H. Raymond. *Historical Records of the 40th (2nd Somersetshire) Regiment*. Devonport: A. H. Swiss, 1894.
65. Lomax, Lt. and Adj. D. A. N. *A History of the Services of the 41st (The Welch) Regiment*. Devonport: 1899. Chapter XI, "Notes on the Uniform and Equipment," by S. M. Milne, pp. 333-34.
66. *Ibid*.
67. Noted at The Royal Green Jackets Museum, 16/3/90.
68. National Army Museum, unscheduled material among the archives in the Gaunt Collection*.
69. W&W 169, 8/70.
70. The Royal Green Jackets Museum, 16/3/90.
71. Gaunt Collection.
72. Author's collection.
73. Ivall and Thomas, *op cit*.
74. *Ibid*.
75. Photograph from Mr R. G. Harris.
76. Gaunt Collection.
77. W&W 169, 8/70.
78. W&W 169, 8/70.
79. Author's collection.
80. W&W 169, 8/70.
81. Gaunt Collection.
82. Mr John Atkin's collection.
83. Mr John Atkin's collection.
84. Army Museums Ogilby Trust.
85. Gaunt Collection.
86. Soldier Shop Catalogue.

* Hereinafter referred to as "Gaunt Collection".

Figure
87. Photograph from Mr R. G. Harris.
88. W&W Luscombe Sale, 12/72 — 1/73.
89. The Essex Regiment Museum, 20/3/91.
90. National Army Museum, 20/3/93.
91. Photograph from Mr R. G. Harris.
92. Photograph from Mr C. Housley.
93. Sketch from Mr W. Y. Carman.
94. W&W 300, 2/85.
95. Collection of the late Mr H. Y. Usher.
96. Cook, Colonel H. C. B., *op cit*.
97. Gaunt Collection.
98. Gaunt Collection.
99. W&W 169, 8/70.
100. Gaunt Collection.
101. Gaunt Collection.
102. Mr John Atkin's collection.
103. Gaunt Collection.
104. Leaflet published by The Durham Light Infantry Museum and Arts Council, 1980.
105. Photograph from Mr R. G. Harris.
106. W&W 169, 8/70.
107. Mr John Atkin's collection.
108. Dealer's list, 1977.
109. W&W 280, 12/82.
110. Gaunt Collection.
111. Kent Sales, 156, 11/78.
112. Dealer's list, 1978.
113. W&W 294, 6/84.
114. W&W 169, 8/70.
115. Gaunt Collection.
116. W&W 289, 12/83.
117. Cook, Colonel H. C. B., *op. cit*.
118. Photocopy from Mr W. Y. Carman.
119. W&W 169, 8/70.
120. Admiral Whiteside's collection.
121. Field Marshal Sir John Chapple's collection.
122. Soldier Shop Catalogue.
123. Parfitt, G. Archer. "Regimental Music of the Corps of the King's Shropshire Light Infantry," *The Bulletin*, The Military Historical Society, Vol. XVII, No. 68, May 1967, Plate II.
124. Gaunt Collection.
125. Gaunt Collection.
126. Photograph from Mr R. G. Harris.
127. Gaunt Collection.
128. Field Marshal Sir John Chapple's collection.
129. Field Marshal Sir John Chapple's collection.
130. Gaunt Collection.
131. Gaunt Collection.
132. Photograph from Mr R. G. Harris.
133. Williams, J. Robert. "The Coronet Badge of the 89th," *The Bulletin*, The Military Historical Society, Vol. XXXX, No. 158, November 1989.
134. The collection of the late Captain Philippe Durand.
135. Taylor, M. E. "91st Argyllshire Highlanders," *Dispatch*, The Journal of the Scottish Military Collectors' Society.
136. Gaunt Collection.
137. Gaunt Collection.
138. Gaunt Collection.

Figure
139. Collection of the late Mr H. Y. Usher.
140. Gaunt Collection.
141. W&W 273, 3/82.
142. Gaunt Collection.
143. W&W 169, 8/70.
144. Gaunt Collection.
145. Gaunt Collection.
146. Field Marshal Sir John Chapple's collection.
147. Photograph from Mr R. G. Harris.
148. W&W 293, 5/84.
149. Photograph from Mr R. G. Harris.
150. W&W Special Spring Sale, 5/88.
151. W&W Special Spring Sale, 5/88.
152. Field Marshal Sir John Chapple's collection.
153. Photograph from Mr R. G. Harris.
154. W&W Connoisseur Collectors' Autumn Sale, 11/91.
155. Mr John Atkin's collection.
156. Leaflet published by The Durham Light Infantry Museum and Arts Council, 1980.
157. Photocopy from the Sussex Combined Services Museum.
158. Speculation.
159. Author's collection.
160. Gaunt Collection.
161. Gaunt Collection.
162. Author's collection.
163. Photocopy from Mr Charles Quinn.
164. Photograph from Mr R. G. Harris.
165. Admiral Whiteside's collection.
166. Wood, Colonel D. R. *The Fifth Fusiliers and Its Badges*. London: published by the author, 1988.
167. *Ibid*.
168. William Dowler's pattern book, courtesy of Mr Hugh King.
169. Mr John Atkin's collection.
170. Admiral Whiteside's collection.
171. W&W 315, 10/86.
172. Photograph from Mr R. G. Harris.
173. Author's collection.
174. Admiral Whiteside's collection.
175. Author's collection.
176. Author's collection.
177. Author's collection.
178. Author's collection.
179. Author's collection.
180. Photocopy from Mr Charles Quinn.
181. Admiral Whiteside's collection.
182. Photograph from Mr W. Y. Carman.
183. Field Marshal Sir John Chapple's collection.
184. Author's collection.
185. Collins, Brigadier T. F. J., CBE. "Officers' Belt Lockets of the Green Howards," *Journal of the Society for Army Historical Research*, Vol XXXVII, pp. 161ff.
186. Author's collection.
187. Photograph from Mr R. G. Harris.
188. Photograph from Mr R. G. Harris.
189. W&W Luscombe Sale, 12/72-1/73.
190. Notes made by the late Mr E. A. Campbell.
191. Author's collection.
192. Mr John Atkin's collection.

Figure
193. Author's collection.
194. Author's collection.
195. Mr John Atkin's collection.
196. Pereira, Captain H. P. E., *op. cit.* Figure 118.
197. Author's collection.
198. Author's collection.
199. Photograph from Mr R. G. Harris.
200. Photograph from Mr R. G. Harris.
201. Author's collection.
202. Photograph from Mr R. G. Harris.
203. Captain Durand's collection.
204. Captain Durand's collection.
205. Author's collection.
206. Photocopy from Mr Charles Quinn.
207. Author's collection.
208. Author's collection.
209. Mr John Atkin's collection.
210. Soldier Shop Catalogue.
211. Author's collection.
212. Author's collection.
213. Author's collection.
214. Photocopy from Mr Charles Quinn.
215. Photograph from Mr R. G. Harris.
216. W&W 289, 12/83.
217. Photograph from Mr R. G. Harris.
218. Mr John Atkin's collection.
219. Mr John Atkin's collection.
220. Photograph from Mr R. G. Harris.
221. Mr John Atkin's collection.
222. Photograph from Mr R. G. Harris.
223. Parfitt, G. Archer, *op. cit.*
224. *Ibid.*
225. Author's collection.
226. Photograph from Mr R. G. Harris.
227. Mr H. Y. Usher's collection.
228. Author's collection.
229. Photograph from Mr R. G. Harris.
230. Mr John Atkin's collection.
231. Photograph from Colonel D. R. Wood.
232. Author's collection.
233. Field Marshal Sir John Chapple's collection.
234. Photograph from Mr R. G. Harris.
235. Field Marshal Sir John Chapple's collection.
236. Field Marshal Sir John Chapple's collection.
237. Photograph from Mr R. G. Harris.
238. Author's collection.
239. W&W Special Sale, 5/88.
240. Photograph from Mr R. G. Harris.
241. Author's collection.